Marc Chagall
Tapestries Tapisserien Tapisseries

Jacob Baal-Teshuva

TASCHEN

KÖLN LONDON MADRID NEW YORK PARIS TOKYO

Marc Chagall
Tapestries

Marc Chagall
Tapisserien

Tapestry, the art of weaving decorative textiles, is one of the most ancient artistic forms. It was widespread in the early Babylonian, Persian, Egyptian and Indian civilisations, as well as in Ancient Greece, where tapestries adorned the walls of the Parthenon, in pre-Columbian Peru, and among tribes such as the Navajo Indians.

Tapestries have been produced down the ages in many different cultures, for the aristocracy and for ordinary citizens. They were used to cover and decorate the walls and floors of public and private places, and even for clothing. The weavers of those tapestries were regarded by their contemporaries as innovative artist-craftsmen, who with skill and patience, and by various techniques, took the designs of other artists on paper or canvas and transformed them into richly coloured textiles.

Some of the earliest and most beautiful tapestries were woven in the 5th and 6th centuries by the Copts in Egypt (ill. p. 5). Their looms consisted of a simple frame with a roller at each end. In the Middle Ages, when tapestry weaving became an important form of employment, new techniques were developed to create illusions of light and shade. During the Renaissance, weavers succeeded in reproducing every brush stroke and nuance of the image by a skilled mixing of dyes.

Colour has always been a central element in tapestry weaving, and the dye master's profession was a highly specialised one. Before the development of chemical dyes, colouring substances were extracted from insects, plants, flowers, shells, onion skins, lemon peel and saffron.

Wool is the material most frequently found in tapestries, although other fibres such as cotton, silk and linen are also common. The Peruvians used fine alpaca and silky vicuna wool, the Copts favoured linen, and the Chinese silk. Down the ages, the predominant subjects portrayed in tapestries have been religious motifs and scenes from myths and legends.

The age-old art of tapestry weaving flourished right up into the 20th century. In the 1930s the French weaver Mme. Marie Cuttoli gave the craft new impetus

Die Kunst, dekorative Wandteppiche zu weben, ist eine der ältesten Formen der bildenden Kunst. Sie war in frühen Kulturen wie der babylonischen, persischen, ägyptischen und indischen ebenso verbreitet wie im alten Griechenland, wo Bildteppiche die Wände des Parthenon schmückten, im vorkolumbianischen Peru und bei den Navajo-Indianern.

In allen Epochen und vielen verschiedenen Kulturen wurden prachtvolle Tapisserien hergestellt, nicht nur für die Aristokratie, sondern auch für den gewöhnlichen Bürger. Sie bedeckten und schmückten die Wände und Böden öffentlicher und privater Räume und wurden sogar als Kleidungsstücke verwendet. Die Weber dieser Tapisserien wurden von ihren Zeitgenossen als innovative Künstler betrachtet, die das, was andere Künstler auf Papier oder Leinwand entworfen hatten, mit großer Kunstfertigkeit und Geduld und mittels unterschiedlicher Techniken in farbenprächtige Bildteppiche übertrugen.

Einige der frühesten und schönsten Tapisserien wurden im 5. und 6. Jahrhundert n. Chr. von den Kopten in Ägypten gefertigt (Abb. S. 5). Ihr Webstuhl bestand aus einem einfachen Rahmen mit einer Walze an beiden Enden. Im Mittelalter, als die Teppichweberei zu einem wichtigen Erwerbszweig wurde, wurden neue Techniken entwickelt, um Licht- und Schattenwirkungen zu erreichen. In der Renaissance gelang es den Webern dann, durch eine geschickte Mischung der Farben jeden Pinselstrich und alle Nuancen der Vorlage wiederzugeben.

Die Farbe war immer ein zentrales Element in der Bildweberei, und die Färber waren hochspezialisierte Fachleute. Vor der Entwicklung chemischer Farbstoffe wurden die Farben aus Insekten, Pflanzen, Blumen, Muscheln, Zwiebelschalen, Zitronenschalen und Safran hergestellt.

Für Tapisserien wird hauptsächlich Wolle verwendet, doch auch andere Fasern wie Baumwolle, Seide und Leinen sind nicht selten zu finden. Die Peruaner verwendeten feines Alpaka und seidige Vikunjawolle, die Kopten Leinen und die Chinesen Seide. Unter den Sujets herrschen seit alters religiöse Motive und Darstellungen von Mythen und Legenden vor.

Marc Chagall
Tapisseries

La tapisserie, en tant que mode de tissage visant à créer des tableaux et représentations décoratives, est l'une des formes artistiques les plus anciennes. On en trouvait déjà à Babylone, en Perse, en Égypte, en Inde, ainsi que dans la Grèce antique, notamment sur les murs du Parthénon, ou au Pérou, à l'ère précolombienne, et chez les Indiens Navajos.

Toutes les époques et les civilisations ont produit de somptueuses tapisseries, tant pour l'aristocratie que pour la bourgeoisie. Elles recouvraient et ornaient les murs et les sols d'intérieurs privés ou publics, et étaient même employées dans le domaine vestimentaire. Les tisserands étaient considérés comme de grands artistes et novateurs qui, au moyen de différentes techniques et avec une infinie patience, rendaient sous forme de magnifiques tapis ce que d'autres artistes transposaient sur le papier ou sur la toile.

Certaines des tapisseries les plus belles et les plus anciennes furent réalisées par les Coptes, en Égypte, aux Vᵉ et VIᵉ siècles après J.-C. (ill. p. 6). Leur métier à tisser consistait tout simplement en un cadre avec une roulette à chaque extrémité. Plus tard, au Moyen Âge, quand le tissage des tapisseries devint un véritable artisanat, de nouvelles techniques furent élaborées pour créer des effets d'ombre et de lumière. À la Renaissance, les tisserands reproduisaient sur la tapisserie chaque coup de pinceau et chaque nuance de l'image en mélangeant habilement les couleurs. La couleur fut de tout temps un élément essentiel du tissage, et le maître teinturier un très grand spécialiste. Avant les teintures chimiques, les couleurs étaient produites à partir d'insectes, de végétaux, coquillages, pelures d'oignons, écorces de citrons et safran.

En tapisserie, c'est surtout la laine qui est utilisée, quoique l'on rencontre fréquemment d'autres fibres, comme le coton, la soie et le lin — ainsi le poil fin de l'alpaga et le poil soyeux de la vigogne chez les Péruviens, le lin chez les Coptes et la soie chez les Chinois. Les sujets et les motifs étaient généralement empruntés aux peintures religieuses, aux légendes et aux mythes.

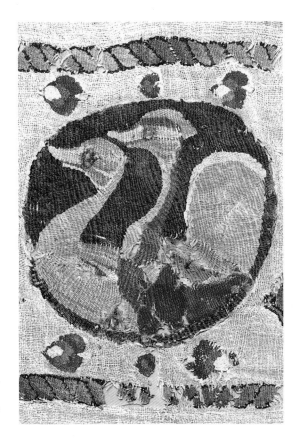

Coptic tapestry (Egypt),
6th–7th century BC
Koptische Tapisserie (Ägypten)
Tapisserie copte (Égypte)

Tapestry
31.5 x 22.5 cm
Musée national du Moyen Âge, Thermes de Cluny, Paris

Animal Tales (detail), 1991
Tiererzählungen (Detail)
Le Bestiaire (détail)

Tapestry (unique piece),
manufactured by master-craftswoman
Yvette Cauquil-Prince after the painting
"Animals and Music", 1969
420 x 435 cm
Private collection
Photo: Claude Gaspari

by commissioning famous contemporary artists such as
Picasso, Braque, Derain, Rouault, Miró, Raoul Dufy and
Le Corbusier to create cartoons for tapestries. Then, in
the second half of the 20th century, new techniques and
artistic approaches to tapestry weaving were developed.
A leading light in this field was Yvette Cauquil-Prince, a
master-craftswoman who produced fascinating tapestries also from the designs of leading artists, including
Picasso (ill. p. 20–21), Léger, Braque, Kandinsky, Klee
(ill. p. 19), Max Ernst, Alexander Calder and Roberto
Matta. Marc Chagall's interest in this art form – just one
of the many to which he turned his hand during the
course of his long life – began in the early 1960s, when
he was already well into his seventies.

Chagall's tapestries for the Knesset

In February 1962 Chagall visited Jerusalem to attend
the unveiling of his twelve magnificent stained-glass
windows in the synagogue of the Hadassah Medical
Centre. On this occasion, Kadish Luz, the Speaker of the
Knesset (Israeli parliament) at the time, asked him to
take over the decoration of the state reception hall in the
new parliament building, still under construction. The
Israeli Knesset is situated on a hilltop known as Givat
Ram, affording a beautiful panorama of Jerusalem. On
one side there is the Israel Museum, facing the campus
of the Hebrew University, and on the other side several
government buildings, including the Prime Minister's
offices. Originally, stained-glass windows were pro-
posed and later a large mural. However, in the summer
of 1963, Chagall decided that tapestries would best suit
this huge hall, flooded with natural Jerusalem light.
The subject suggested to him for the tapestries was the
History of the Jewish People, from their return to their
homeland, Zion, up to the creation of the State of Israel
in 1948. Chagall accepted the proposition with great
enthusiasm. He decided to do three tapestries and began
straightaway to work on the first cartoon (ill. p. 10–11) –
a preparatory gouache which served as a model for the
tapestry weavers. This first cartoon was presented on
November 30, 1963 in Paris to the world-famous French
tapestry manufacturers : Manufacture nationale des
Gobelins, an institution founded by Louis XIV in 1667.
The state-subsidised factory also received financial
support from the Parisian branch of the Rothschild
family.

Die jahrhundertealte Kunst der Bildweberei blieb auch im 20. Jahrhundert lebendig. In den 30er Jahren gab ihr die Französin Marie Cuttoli einen neuen Auftrieb. Bedeutende zeitgenössische Künstler wie Picasso, Braque, Derain, Rouault, Miró, Raoul Dufy und Le Corbusier schufen in ihrem Auftrag Vorlagen für Tapisserien. In der zweiten Hälfte des 20. Jahrhunderts wurden neue Techniken und neue künstlerische Ansätze eingeführt. Wegbereitend war in dieser Hinsicht Yvette Cauquil-Prince, eine Meisterin der Teppichwebkunst, die nach Entwürfen führender Künstler unseres Jahrhunderts wie Picasso (Abb. S. 20–21), Léger, Braque, Kandinsky, Klee (Abb. S. 19), Max Ernst, Alexander Calder und Roberto Matta faszinierende Bildteppiche schuf.

Marc Chagalls Interesse an dieser Kunstform – nur eine von so vielen, mit denen dieser ungemein vielseitige Künstler sich im Laufe seines langen Lebens beschäftigte – wurde in den frühen 60er Jahren geweckt, als er das 70. Lebensjahr bereits weit überschritten hatte.

Chagalls Tapisserien für die Knesset

Im Februar 1962 besuchte Chagall Jerusalem, um der Enthüllung seiner zwölf prachtvollen Glasfenster für die Synagoge des Hadassah-Klinikums beizuwohnen. Bei dieser Gelegenheit bat ihn Kadish Luz, der damalige Sprecher des israelischen Parlaments, der Knesset, die Dekoration der für Staatsempfänge bestimmten Halle des im Bau befindlichen neuen Parlamentsgebäudes zu übernehmen. Die Knesset liegt auf dem Givat Ram, einem Hügel mit einem herrlichen Blick auf Jerusalem. Auf der einen Seite befinden sich ihm gegenüber das Israel Museum und der Campus der Hebräischen Universität, auf der anderen mehrere Regierungsgebäude, darunter der Sitz des Premierministers. Zunächst wurden Buntglasfenster und später ein großes Wandgemälde in Erwägung gezogen. Im Sommer 1963 kam Chagall jedoch zu der Überzeugung, daß Wandteppiche für diese große, vom Jerusalemer Licht durchflutete Halle am besten geeignet seien. Als Thema wurde ihm die Geschichte des jüdischen Volkes vorgeschlagen, von der Rückkehr nach Zion bis zur Gründung des Staates Israel im Jahre 1948. Chagall griff diese Idee begeistert auf. Er beschloß, drei Tapisserien zu entwerfen und begann gleich mit der Arbeit an dem ersten Karton – der Gouache, die den Teppichwebern als Vorlage dient (Abb. S. 10–11). Dieser Karton wurde am 30. November

L'art de la tapisserie s'est perpétué au fil des temps, jusqu'au XXe siècle. Dans les années trente, la Française Marie Cuttoli s'attacha à lui donner un nouvel essor en incitant les grands artistes de l'époque – Picasso, Braque, Derain, Rouault, Miró, Raoul Dufy, Le Corbusier et d'autres – à en créer. La deuxième moitié du XXe siècle vit apparaître des techniques et approches artistiques nouvelles. Une des plus grandes personnalités à cet égard est Yvette Cauquil-Prince, maître en la matière, qui réalisa de fascinantes tapisseries pour les plus grands artistes du siècle, parmi lesquels Picasso (ill. pp. 20–21), Léger, Braque, Kandinsky, Klee (ill. p. 19), Ernst, Calder et Matta.

L'intérêt de Marc Chagall pour cette forme d'art – parmi tant d'autres qui préoccupèrent cet artiste aux talents multiples – se manifesta au début des années soixante, alors qu'il avait déjà plus de soixante-dix ans.

Les tapisseries pour la Knesset

En février 1962, en visite à Jérusalem pour inaugurer les douze magnifiques vitraux qu'il avait réalisés pour la synagogue de la clinique Hadassah, Chagall fut invité par Kadish Luz, porte-parole de la Knesset, et chargé de la décoration du hall de réception du Parlement, alors en construction. Le bâtiment de la Knesset est situé au sommet d'une colline, connue sous le nom de « Givat Ram » et dominant le superbe panorama de Jérusalem. Il fait face au Israel Museum et au campus de l'université hébraïque d'un côté, et à divers édifices du gouvernement, dont les bureaux du Premier ministre, de l'autre. Il fut d'abord question de réaliser des vitraux, puis on envisagea une grande peinture murale. Au cours de l'été 1963, Chagall décida cependant que des tapisseries conviendraient mieux à ce vaste hall, tout entier inondé de la lumière naturelle de Jérusalem. Le sujet qui lui fut proposé était l'histoire du peuple juif, depuis le retour à Sion jusqu'à la création de l'État d'Israël en 1948. Chagall accepta l'idée avec enthousiasme et décida de réaliser trois tapisseries. Aussitôt il commença à préparer le premier carton (la peinture à la gouache qui sert de modèle aux tisserands ; ill. pp. 10–11). Ce carton fut remis le 30 novembre 1963 à la très célèbre Manufacture nationale des Gobelins. Fondée en 1667 par Louis XIV, l'une des plus anciennes du genre et connue dans le monde entier, elle bénéficia du soutien de la branche française de la famille

The Entry into Jerusalem, 1963–1964
Der Einzug in Jerusalem
L'Entrée à Jérusalem

Preliminary drawing
Pencil and ink
126.7 x 126.7 cm
Private collection

Exodus, 1963
Exodus
L'Exode

Preliminary drawing
Pencil and ink
126.7 x 165.5 cm
Private collection

PAGE/SEITE /PAGE 9
Isaiah's Prophecy, 1963
Die Prophezeiung Jesajas
La Prophétie d'Isaïe

Preliminary drawing
Pencil and ink
126.7 x 126.7 cm
Private collection

In the summer of 1964, after returning from another
visit to Israel, Chagall completed the second and third
cartoons (ill. p. 10–11). It was estimated that the weaving
of the three tapestries would take four years. 160 different shades of colour and 68 kilometres of thread were
needed to reproduce Chagall's gouaches in these huge
wall hangings (ill. p. 24–28). The 120 cm-high cartoons
had to be enlarged nearly four times to reach the required
height of 475 centimetres. Chagall, who was living at
the time in Vence in the South of France, travelled frequently up to Paris to watch the work in progress and
discuss problems with the weavers as they arose. The
weaving of the three tapestries, begun in February 1965,
was finished at the beginning of 1968, a year earlier
than planned. The triptych consists of one 904-cm-wide
tapestry and two smaller, 528-cm and 533-cm-wide
ones, all of the same height, that were hung side by side.
The theme of the largest of the three, in the centre, is
Exodus (ill. p. 26–27), that on the right, *Isaiah's Prophecy*
(ill. p. 28–29) and that on the left, *The Entry into Jerusalem*
(ill. p. 24–25). *Exodus* shows Moses, portrayed by Chagall
in blue, leading the Children of Israel out of Egypt.
Hovering over them is the large cloud that accompanied
them on their long journey and protected them from
their Egyptian pursuers until they had crossed the Red

1963 der weltberühmten, traditionsreichen Pariser Manufacture nationale des Gobelins übergeben, die 1667 von Ludwig XIV. gegründet wurde. Diese staatlich geförderte Manufaktur wurde vom Pariser Zweig der Rothschild-Familie finanziell unterstützt.

Nach einem weiteren Israelbesuch im Sommer 1964 vollendete Chagall den zweiten und dritten Karton (Abb. S. 8–11). Für die Fertigstellung der drei Tapisserien wurden vier Jahre veranschlagt. 160 verschiedene Farbtöne und 68 Kilometer Garn wurden benötigt, um Chagalls Gouachen in große Wandteppiche zu übertragen. Die 120 Zentimeter hohen Kartons mußten fast um das Vierfache vergrößert werden, um die Höhe der Tapserien – 475 Zentimeter – zu erreichen. Chagall, der damals im südfranzösischen Vence lebte, kam häufig nach Paris, um die Fertigung zu überwachen und die dabei auftretenden Probleme mit den Webern zu erörtern. Die im Februar 1965 begonnenen Arbeiten an den drei Teppichen konnten Anfang 1968, ein Jahr früher als geplant, vollendet werden. Das Triptychon besteht aus einem großen, 904 Zentimeter breiten, und zwei kleineren, 528 bzw. 533 Zentimetern breiten Wandteppichen mit derselben Höhe. Auf dem großen Teppich in der Mitte ist der *Exodus* (Abb. S. 26–27) dargestellt, auf dem kleineren rechts davon die *Prophezeiung Jesajas*

Rothschild en association avec le gouvernement français.

Après un nouveau voyage en Israël à l'été 1964, Chagall termina les deux autres cartons (ill. pp. 10–11). On estima alors qu'il faudrait quatre années pour achever les trois tapisseries. 160 teintes différentes et 68 kilomètres de fil furent nécessaires au report des gouaches de Chagall. Les cartons de 120 cm de haut durent être agrandis de presque quatre fois leur taille, afin d'atteindre la hauteur des tapisseries (475 cm). Chagall, qui vivait alors à Vence, dans le Sud de la France, se rendit plusieurs fois à Paris pour assister à l'élaboration de l'œuvre et discuter avec les tisserands des problèmes qui survenaient au fur et à mesure. Le travail sur les trois tapisseries débuta en février 1965 et fut terminé au début de l'année 1968, un an plus tôt que prévu. Le triptyque se compose d'une grande tapisserie de 904 cm de large et de deux plus petites (de 528 et 533 cm), toutes de la même hauteur, accrochées sur une seule ligne. La grande tapisserie, au centre, représente *L'Exode* (ill. pp. 26–27) ; celle de droite, *La Prophétie d'Isaïe* (ill. pp. 28–29) et celle de gauche, *L'Entrée à Jérusalem* (ill. pp. 24–25). La tapisserie centrale montre Moïse, peint en bleu par Chagall et conduisant les enfants d'Israël hors d'Égypte. Un gros nuage au-dessus d'eux

9

The Entry into Jerusalem, 1963–1964
Der Einzug in Jerusalem
L'Entrée à Jérusalem

Gouache and drawing
126.7 x 144.7 cm
Private collection

Exodus, 1963
Exodus
L'Exode

Gouache and drawing
126.7 x 165.5 cm
Private collection

PAGE/SEITE /PAGE 11
Isaiah's Prophecy, 1963
Die Prophezeiung Jesajas
La Prophétie d'Isaïe

Gouache and drawing
126.7 x 144.5 cm
Private collection

Sea. The angel blowing the shofar, or ram's horn, over the cloud has been sent by divine providence to guide them on their way. The tapestry is full of symbols and references to biblical events, such as Abraham sacrificing Isaac, and Moses receiving the Ten Commandments on two tablets on the right of the picture. Higher up, one can see the Golden Calf and Jacob wrestling with the Angel. More recent events such as pogroms, the burning of houses, and memories of the Holocaust were also incorporated into the work. The figure of the wandering Jew with a sack on his back is a reference to Chagall's exile in the United States during the Second World War. The central theme, however, is the return of the Jews to their Holy, Promised Land - Israel. This monumental wall hanging is dominated by two great biblical figures: Moses, receiving the Ten Commandments, and King David, playing on his harp. These two themes recur again and again in Chagall's biblical works, including the monumental paintings he did for his own museum, the Musée National Message Biblique Marc Chagall in Nice (ill. p. 58–59).

To the left of Exodus is the Entry into Jerusalem, the site of the Jewish Temple and the capital of Israel. The central figure of King David playing the harp, in red regalia and crown, makes this tapestry an obvious continuation of the narrative beside it. A festive scene is

(Abb. S. 28–29) und links der *Einzug in Jerusalem* (Abb. S. 24–25). *Exodus* zeigt Moses – von Chagall in blauer Farbe ausgeführt –, der die Kinder Israels aus Ägypten führt. Über ihnen schwebt eine große Wolke, die sie auf ihrer langen Reise leitet und vor den ägyptischen Verfolgern schützt, bevor sie das Rote Meer durchqueren. Der Engel, der über der Wolke den Schofar (das Widderhorn) bläst, ist von der göttlichen Vorsehung gesandt worden, um sie auf ihrer Reise zu führen. Der Wandteppich ist angefüllt mit biblischen Ereignissen und Symbolen. So sind zum Beispiel rechts das Opfer Abrahams und die Übergabe der Zehn Gebote auf zwei Tafeln zu sehen. Das Goldene Kalb ist ebenso dargestellt wie Jakobs Ringkampf mit dem Engel. Chagall hat auch Ereignisse aus neuerer Zeit wie Pogrome, brennende Häuser und Erinnerungen an den Holocaust integriert. Das Symbol des wandernden Juden mit einem Bündel auf dem Rücken gemahnt an Chagalls Exil in den Vereinigten Staaten während des Zweiten Weltkriegs. Das zentrale Thema ist jedoch die Rückkehr der Juden in ihr Heiliges und Gelobtes Land – Israel. Dominiert wird dieser monumentale Wandteppich von zwei großen biblischen Gestalten: Moses, der die Zehn Gebote empfängt, und König David, der auf seiner Harfe spielt. Auf diese Sujets griff Chagall im Laufe seines langen Lebens oft zurück, wenn er die Bibel illustrierte, so zum Beispiel

doit les accompagner dans leur long voyage en les protégeant de leurs persécuteurs égyptiens, avant de traverser la mer Rouge. Un ange soufflant dans le schofar (la corne de bélier), au-dessus du nuage, est envoyé par la divine providence pour les guider dans leur périple. La tapisserie abonde en événements et symboles bibliques, tels le sacrifice d'Isaac par Abraham ou les Dix Commandements sur deux tables, le Veau d'Or ou Jacob luttant avec l'Ange. Chagall y a aussi placé des événements contemporains, comme les pogroms, les maisons incendiées ou d'autres éléments devant rappeler l'Holocauste. Le symbole du Juif errant avec un sac sur le dos évoque l'exil de Chagall aux États-Unis pendant la Deuxième Guerre mondiale. Mais le thème central demeure le retour des Juifs en Terre promise : Israël. Deux grandes figures bibliques dominent cette monumentale tapisserie : Moïse recevant les Dix Commandements et le roi David jouant de sa harpe. Chagall traita ces motifs de nombreuses fois tout au long de sa carrière artistique, dans ses illustrations de la Bible ou dans les monumentales peintures exposées en permanence dans son Musée National Message Biblique, à Nice (ill. pp. 58–59).

À gauche de *L'Exode*, on peut voir *L'Entrée à Jérusalem*, capitale éternelle de Jérusalem abritant le temple juif. Avec le roi David jouant de la harpe, cette tapisserie perpétue le thème de la précédente. La scène, qui dégage

portrayed with many figures playing musical instruments, beating drums and blowing horns. In their midst the Ark of the Covenant can be seen. To the left you find the Israeli flag with the Star of David and "Israel" written in Hebrew. In this magnificent tapestry, with its magical colours, Chagall combines biblical history, the present, and the future.

The three tapestries draw together the main elements of Jewish history relating to the foundation of the State of Israel. While *Exodus* shows the handing over of the tablets of the Law to Moses and the suffering throughout history of the Jewish People, *The Entry into Jerusalem* portrays the triumphal entry of King David into Zion and the return of the Jewish people to their ancestral homeland. The third tapestry, to the right of *Exodus*, entitled *Isaiah's Prophecy* depicts the idyllic vision of the prophet Isaiah. Chagall has translated the Bible passage into pictorial language, word for word: "and the wolf shall dwell with the lamb, and the leopard shall lie down with the kid; and the calf and the young lion and the fatling shall graze together; and a little child shall lead them." (Isaiah 11, 6)

These three tapestries, with their powerful imagery, constituted a huge triumph for Chagall. They were a testament to his successful collaboration with the weavers, whose faithful rendering of all the many blue, green, red, gold, yellow, brown, purple and white colours of his cartoons was a great accomplishment. All three tapestries bear the date of completion and are signed by the artist and the weavers involved.

The triptych was officially unveiled with great ceremony on June 18, 1969 in the presence of the artist, the then President of Israel, Zalman Shazar, Prime Minister Golda Meir, and the Knesset Speaker Kadish Luz (p. 13). In his speech, Chagall said that these works had been inspired by the founding of the State of Israel, that they represented a kindling of "new hope" and that he had put into them "the experience, the suffering and the joy of a whole lifetime". "My aim was to get closer to the biblical homeland of the Jewish people, to the land where the creative spirit, the Holy Spirit, is at home, such as hovers over every page of the Bible; and hovers here in the air, over the fields and in the hearts and souls of the inhabitants [...] Works of genius and luminosity are so rare [...] People prefer to be content with evil and injustice than to reach out with love [...] There is no art

auch in den monumentalen Gemälden biblischer Szenen für sein Musée National Message Biblique Marc Chagall in Nizza (Abb. S. 58–59).

Links neben *Exodus* ist der *Einzug in Jerusalem* zu sehen, der Heimstatt des jüdischen Tempels und der ewigen Hauptstadt Israels. Mit der zentralen Figur des gekrönten und in königlichem Rot gekleideten, Harfe spielenden König David führt dieser Wandteppich das Thema des mittleren unverkennbar fort. Dargestellt ist eine festliche Szene mit vielen Musikinstrumente spielenden, Trommeln schlagenden und Hörner blasenden Figuren. Inmitten dieser Figuren ist die Bundeslade zu sehen. Links sieht man die Staatsflagge Israels mit dem Davidstern und dem Namen Israel in hebräischer Schrift.

Die drei Wandteppiche stellen eine Zusammenfassung der zur Gründung des Staates Israel führenden jüdischen Geschichte dar. Während *Exodus* die Überreichung der Gesetzestafeln an Moses und die leidensvolle Geschichte des jüdischen Volkes und *Einzug in Jerusalem* den triumphalen Einzug König Davids in Zion und die Rückkehr des jüdischen Volkes in seine angestammte Heimat zeigt, schildert der dritte, rechts von *Exodus* zu sehende Wandteppich, die *Prophezeiung Jesajas*, die idyllische Zukunft, die dieser Prophet der Welt vorhergesagt hat. Wortwörtlich folgt Chagall hier dem biblischen Text: »Dann wohnt der Wolf beim Lamm, der Panther liegt beim Böcklein. Kalb und Löwe weiden zusammen, ein kleiner Knabe kann sie hüten.« (Jesaja 11,6).

Mit ihrer beeindruckenden Bildsprache bedeuteten diese drei Tapisserien für Chagall einen großen Triumph. Sie bezeugen die erfolgreiche Zusammenarbeit zwischen ihm und den Webern, die die vielen verschiedenen Blau-, Grün-, Rot-, Gold-, Gelb-, Braun-, Lila- und Weißtöne seiner Kartons originalgetreu übertrugen und damit eine großartige Leistung vollbrachten. Alle drei Wandteppiche tragen das Datum ihrer Vollendung und sind von Chagall und den beteiligten Webern signiert.

Die drei Wandteppiche wurden am 18. Juni 1969 in Anwesenheit des Künstlers, des damaligen israelischen Staatspräsidenten, Salman Schasar, der Ministerpräsidentin Golda Meir und des Parlamentssprechers Kadish Luz in einer feierlichen Zeremonie offiziell enthüllt (Abb. S. 13). In seiner Rede sagte Chagall, daß diese Werke durch die Gründung des Staates Israel inspiriert

œuvre exprime tout mon amour pour mon pays, terre de justice et de paix biblique. »

Les trois tapisseries sont pleines d'harmonie et d'inspiration ; elles illustrent à merveille les propos de Chagall : « Je suis contre des termes comme ‹ imagination › et ‹ symbolisme ›. Tout notre monde intérieur est réel, peut-être même plus réel que le monde visible. » Pour Chagall, il s'agissait là d'une toute nouvelle expérience, et ces tapisseries furent unanimement considérées comme des chefs-d'œuvre du genre. Elles constituent une véritable symphonie de couleurs, que lui seul pouvait rendre ainsi — lui qui, tout au long de sa riche carrière artistique, avait tant traité les motifs religieux : « Il faut avoir mon âge pour pouvoir réaliser une œuvre comme celle-ci. »

Les tapisseries de Chagall pour la Knesset, célèbres dans le monde entier, expriment toute l'admiration de l'artiste pour l'extraordinaire accomplissement par le peuple juif de la prophétie biblique sur la résurrection d'Israël. Les couleurs, la lumière, le rythme, radieux et magiques, qui se manifestent dans cette monumentale réalisation, illustrent avec force et grandeur , sa foi en Israël et dans le peuple juif.

Marc Chagall with Yvette Cauquil-Prince, c. 1966
Marc Chagall mit Yvette Cauquil-Prince, ca. 1966
Marc Chagall avec Yvette Cauquil-Prince, vers 1966

La tapisserie pour le Musée National Message Biblique Marc Chagall

En 1969, André Malraux, célèbre ministre de la Culture et homme de lettres, qualifia Marc Chagall de dernier héros de l'art du XXe siècle et lui dédia un musée national, six ans seulement après que Chagall fut chargé de peindre le plafond de l'Opéra du Palais Garnier, à Paris. Pour Malraux, Chagall était « l'un des plus grands coloristes de notre temps, l'un des plus grands artistes du siècle ». On opta pour Cimiez, à Nice, et la première pierre du Musée National Message Biblique Marc Chagall fut posée en 1969. Le fonds du musée était constitué d'une série de 17 peintures monumentales que l'artiste avait données à l'État français. Pour le musée, Chagall réalisa également plusieurs vitraux et une mosaïque, mais l'une des œuvres les plus saisissantes est la tapisserie de l'entrée qui fut tissée à la Manufacture nationale des Gobelins, à Paris (ill. pp. 58–59). Cette tapisserie de 226 cm sur 322 cm, la quatrième tissée à la Manufacture, dépeint en des tons de jaune, rouge, brun et bleu, des scènes de Nice avec les palmiers et la mer. Le musée ouvrit ses portes le

at that factory. The 226 x 322 cm work in bright yellows, reds, browns and blues, depicts Nice, with its palm trees and sea. The museum was opened on 7 July 1973, Chagall's 86th birthday. It is dedicated to the message of the Bible, which remained close to Chagall's heart all his life: "Ever since early childhood, I have been captivated by the Bible. It has always seemed to me, and still seems to me today, to be the greatest source of poetry of all time. Ever since then, I have searched for its reflection in life and in art. The Bible is like an echo of nature, and this is the secret I have tried to convey."

The tapestries of Yvette Cauquil-Prince

In 1964, while he was in Paris supervising the weaving of his Knesset tapestries, Chagall was introduced by Mme. Madeleine Malraux, the French Minister of Culture's wife, to Yvette Cauquil-Prince, one of the most famous tapestry weavers of our time and an absolute master of this revered and ancient craft. Her works were already acclaimed by experts and curators of important museums all over the world, including the Louvre. "The tapestry universe conveyed by Yvette Cauquil-Prince takes on a new significance; it is a new creation, another aspect of the work, its natural continuation", observed Jean-Louis Prat, director of the Maeght Foundation in Saint-Paul-de-Vence. "Nothing is identical with the original", he continued, "everything is different and complementary, for tapestry demands other lines of force provided by a creative autonomy: the autonomy of the master-craftswoman [...] that is why Chagall was so happy to have his own creation reinvented by this intermediary."

Yvette Cauquil-Prince exhibited her tapestries in museums as far afield as Japan, Finland, Spain and the United States, some forming part of permanent collections there. Her rendering of Picasso's *La Minotauromachie* (ill. p. 20) – composed only in the colours of black, white and grey – is a masterpiece that leaves the viewer spellbound. Here she managed to transform Picasso's black and white etching, with all its nuances of light and shade, into a monumental mural. In all her tapestries one senses her great love of the artist and his original creation. In the words of Sylvie Forestier, former director of the Musée National Message Biblique Marc Chagall in Nice, "the thread never betrays the brush; on the contrary, everything that is expressed in the pictorial

größte Bildschöpfer des Jahrhunderts.« In Cimiez, in den Hügeln bei Nizza wurde ein geeignetes Gelände gefunden, und 1969 wurde der Grundstein für das künftige Musée National Message Biblique Marc Chagall gelegt. Die Basis des Museums bildete eine Folge von 17 monumentalen Gemälden, die der Künstler dem französischen Staat schenkte. Chagall schuf mehrere Buntglasfenster und ein Mosaik für sein Museum, doch eines der eindrucksvollsten Werke ist der Wandteppich für die Eingangshalle (Abb. S. 58–59), der in der Manufacture nationale des Gobelins in Paris gewebt wurde . Er war der vierte und letzte Wandteppich Chagalls, der in dieser Manufaktur gefertigt wurde. Der 226 x 322 Zentimeter große und mit seinen Gelb-, Rot-, Braun- und Blautönen farbenfrohe Wandteppich zeigt Nizza mit seinen Palmen und dem Meer. Am 7. Juli 1973, Chagalls 86. Geburtstag, wurde das Museum eröffnet. Es ist der Botschaft der Bibel gewidmet, die Chagall zeitlebens besonders am Herzen lag: »Seit meiner frühesten Jugend hat mich die Bibel gefesselt. Die Bibel schien mir – und scheint mir heute noch – die reichste poetische Quelle aller Zeiten zu sein. Seither habe ich ihr Abbild im Leben und in der Kunst gesucht. Die Bibel ist wie ein Nachklang der Natur, und dieses Geheimnis habe ich weiterzugeben versucht.«

Die Tapisserien von Yvette Cauquil-Prince

Als in der Manufacture nationale des Gobelins die Tapisserien für die Knesset gewebt wurden, kam Chagall häufig nach Paris, um die Arbeiten zu überwachen und technische Probleme zu lösen. 1964 wurde er von Madeleine Malraux, der Gattin des damaligen französischen Kulturministers, mit Yvette Cauquil-Prince bekannt gemacht. Sie gehört zu den bedeutendsten Künstlerinnen unserer Zeit, die die altehrwürdige Kunst der Bildweberei souverän beherrscht. Ihre Arbeit wurde von Experten und Kuratoren bedeutender Museen wie etwa des Louvre gepriesen. »Das von Yvette Cauquil-Prince vermittelte Spektrum der Tapisserie [...] ist eine neue Schöpfung, ein anderer Aspekt des Werks, dessen natürliche Weiterführung«, sagte Jean-Louis Prat, der Direktor der Fondation Maeght in Saint-Paul-de-Vence. »Nichts ist mit dem Original identisch«, so führte er weiter aus, »alles ist anders und komplementär, denn die Bildteppichkunst verlangt andere Kraftlinien, für die es einer kreativen Autonomie bedarf: der Autonomie der Gobe-

7 juillet 1973, le jour des 86 ans de Chagall ; il est dédié au message biblique qui a occupé une place centrale dans la vie de l'artiste : « Depuis ma plus tendre jeunesse, j'ai été captivé par la Bible. Elle m'a toujours paru, et aujourd'hui encore, comme la plus grande source de poésie de tous les temps. Je cherche depuis son reflet dans la vie et dans l'art. La Bible est comme l'écho de la nature, et c'est ce secret que j'ai essayé de transmettre. »

Les tapisseries d' Yvette Cauquil-Prince

Tandis que la Manufacture nationale des Gobelins tissait les tapisseries pour la Knesset, Chagall se rendit fréquemment à Paris pour surveiller les travaux et aider à résoudre les problèmes techniques. En 1964, il fit la connaissance d'Yvette Cauquil-Prince qui lui fut présentée par Madeleine Malraux, l'épouse du ministre. Yvette Cauquil-Prince, dont la maîtrise faisait l'admiration de tous les experts et conservateurs de musées, était pour son époque l'une des plus grandes spécialistes de la tapisserie. « L'univers de la tapisserie acquiert grâce à Yvette Cauquil-Prince une signification nouvelle. C'est une nouvelle création, un autre aspect de l'œuvre, c'est une continuation naturelle », déclara Jean-Louis Prat, directeur de la Fondation Maeght à Saint-Paul-de-Vence. « Rien n'est identique à l'original, poursuit M. Prat, tout est différent et complémentaire, car l'art de la tapisserie suppose d'autres lignes de force pour lesquelles il faut une autonomie créative : l'autonomie propre au contremaître... C'est pourquoi Marc Chagall fut si heureux d'avoir pu confier sa création à cette personne qui sut la retransmettre. »

Les tapisseries d'Yvette Cauquil-Prince étaient exposées dans divers musées, du Japon à la Finlande, des États-Unis à l'Espagne, où certaines faisaient même partie des collections permanentes. Sa tapisserie d'après *La Minotauromachie* de Picasso, composée uniquement de tons blancs, noirs et gris (ill. p. 20), est un chef-d'œuvre tout à fait admirable. De fait, cette tapisserie monumentale rend à merveille toutes les nuances de clair-obscur de la gravure en noir et blanc de Picasso. Toutes les tapisseries d'Yvette Cauquil-Prince expriment un profond respect pour l'œuvre originale de l'artiste. Selon Sylvie Forestier, ancienne directrice du Musée National Message Biblique Marc Chagall à Nice, « le fil ne trahit jamais le pinceau, au contraire, tout ce que l'univers pictural exprime est transposé dans la tapisse-

Yvette Cauquil-Prince in front of the Chagall tapestry "Les Arlequins" (The Harlequins), 1993
Yvette Cauquil-Prince vor dem Chagall-Wandteppich »Les Arlequins« (Die Harlekine)
Yvette Cauquil-Prince devant la tapisserie de Chagall « Les Arlequins »

universe is optimally transposed into a tapestry [...] and Yvette Cauquil-Prince is its mediating angel."

Yvette Cauquil-Prince was born in Belgium, where she studied painting. She trained as a tapestry weaver in Paris and often visited the Musée de Cluny and the Musée des Arts Décoratifs to study medieval French and Flemish tapestry weaving as well as Coptic tapestries. In 1959 she opened her first studio in Paris, developing new techniques with a group of weavers under her direction. Between 1959 and 1961 she worked mainly for Asger Jorn and Pierre Wemaëre. From 1961 she produced tapestries for Alexander Calder, Emile Hecq, François-Xavier Lalanne, Roberto Matta, Jean Piaubert, Niki de Saint-Phalle and Michel Seuphor, and from 1967 onwards also for Georges Braque, Chagall himself, Max Ernst, Wassily Kandinsky, Paul Klee, Henry Miller and Pablo Picasso (ill. p.20–21), who trusted her skills implicitly.

On their first meeting, Yvette Cauquil-Prince showed Chagall one of her Picasso tapestries. Chagall was deeply impressed and asked her straightaway to choose one of his works for transposition into a tapestry. She selected *The Harlequin Family* (ill. p. 43), producing a tapestry measuring 205 x 155 cm from it.

Chagall loved the circus his whole life long and painted circus motifs many times. "For me, the circus is a magic show that appears and disappears like a world. There is a disquieting circus, and a true one. [...] 'Circus' is a magic word, a timeless dancing game where tears and smiles, and the play of arms and legs, take the form of great art [...] The circus seems to me to be the most tragic show on earth, man's most poignant cry across the centuries in his search for amusement and joy. It often takes the form of high poetry [...]."

All Chagall's tapestries are taken from paintings in the style of his late work. Chagall was very pleased with Cauquil-Prince's first tapestry for him on the subject of the circus. It marked the beginning of a twenty-year collaboration, which gave rise to 29 Chagall tapestries, some on a grand scale. Daniel Alcouffe, curator at the Louvre, spoke of the "admiration Cauquil-Prince's work aroused [...] She is happy carrying out her task, and beams with serenity." Bella Meyer, Chagall's granddaughter sees in Mme. Cauquil-Prince's work an "articulated language, one that is direct, frank and clear, emerging like the memory of a myth".

linmeisterin [...] deshalb war Marc Chagall so glücklich, seine Schöpfung dieser Mittlerin anvertraut zu haben.«

Ihr Bildteppich nach Picassos *La Minotauromachie* (Abb. S. 20) – nur aus Schwarz-, Weiß- und Grautönen zusammengesetzt – ist ein Meisterwerk, das dem Betrachter Bewunderung abverlangt. Yvette Cauquil-Prince ist es gelungen, Picassos Schwarzweißradierung mit allen ihren Nuancen und Licht- und Schatteneffekten in einen monumentalen Wandteppich umzusetzen. Aus allen ihren Tapisserien spricht eine tiefe Liebe zur ursprünglichen Schöpfung des Künstlers. Wie Sylvie Forestier, die frühere Leiterin des Musée National Message Biblique Marc Chagall es formulierte: »Der Faden verrät den Pinsel nie, im Gegenteil, alles, was im bildlichen Universum zum Ausdruck kommt, wird optimal in eine Tapisserie übertragen.«

Yvette Cauquil-Prince wurde in Belgien geboren, wo sie Malerei studierte. In Paris ließ sie sich dann zur Teppichweberin ausbilden und studierte im Musée de Cluny und im Musée des Arts Décoratifs im Louvre die französische und flämische Bildteppichkunst des Mittelalters sowie die Tapisserien der Kopten. 1959 eröffnete sie in Paris ihre erste Werkstatt, in der eine Gruppe von Webern unter ihrer Anleitung nach von ihr entwickelten neuen Techniken tätig war. Zwischen 1959 und 1961 arbeitete sie hauptsächlich für Asger Jorn und Pierre Wemaëre. Von 1961 an schuf sie Tapisserien für Alexander Calder, Emile Hecq, François-Xavier Lalanne, Roberto Matta, Jean Piaubert, Niki de Saint-Phalle und Michel Seuphor, und seit 1967 auch für Georges Braque, Marc Chagall, Max Ernst, Wassily Kandinsky, Paul Klee, Henry Miller und Pablo Picasso, der größtes Vertrauen in ihre Arbeit setzte.

Bei ihrer ersten Begegnung mit Marc Chagall zeigte Yvette Cauquil-Prince ihm eine ihrer Picasso-Tapisserien. Chagall war zutiefst beeindruckt und bat sie, eines seiner Werke ihrer Wahl in einen Wandteppich umzusetzen. Sie entschied sich für *Die Harlekinfamilie* (Abb. S. 43). Dieser Wandteppich mißt 205 x 155 Zentimeter.

Chagall liebte zeitlebens den Zirkus und malte viele Zirkusmotive. »Für mich ist der Zirkus ein magisches Schauspiel, das kommt und vergeht wie eine Welt. Es gibt einen beunruhigenden Zirkus, einen wahren. [...] Zirkus ist ein magisches Wort, ein tausendjähriges Spiel, das sich tanzen läßt, dessen Tränen und Lachen,

rie [...] et Yvette Cauquil-Prince est l'ange de cette médiation ».

Yvette Cauquil-Prince est née en Belgique où elle étudia la peinture. À Paris, elle suivit une formation de tisserande et étudia au Musée de Cluny et au Musée des Arts décoratifs les art français et flamand de la tapisserie, ainsi que les tapisseries coptes. Elle ouvrit son premier atelier à Paris en 1959 et rassembla sous sa direction un groupe de tisserands travaillant d'après les nouvelles techniques qu'elle avait élaborées. Entre 1959 et 1961, elle travailla surtout pour Asger Jorn et Pierre Wemaëre. À partir de 1961, elle créa des tapisseries pour Alexander Calder, Émile Hecq, François-Xavier Lalanne, Roberto Matta, Jean Piaubert, Niki de Saint-Phalle et Michel Seuphor, puis, à partir de 1967, aussi pour Georges Braque, Marc Chagall, Max Ernst, Vassily Kandinsky, Paul Klee (ill. p. 19), Henry Miller et Pablo Picasso, (ill. pp. 10–21), qui avait une très grande confiance en son travail.

Lors de sa première rencontre avec Marc Chagall, Yvette Cauquil-Prince lui montra une tapisserie d'après Picasso. Chagall fut profondément impressionné et la pria de choisir parmi ses œuvres celle qu'elle souhaiterait transposer en tapisserie. Elle opta pour *La Famille d'Arlequin* (ill. p. 36). Cette tapisserie mesure 205 cm sur 155 cm.

Chagall avait toujours aimé le cirque et en peignit de nombreux motifs. « C'est un monde magique, un cirque, une danse hors du temps où les larmes et les sourires, les jeux de bras et de jambes, prennent la forme d'un grand art [...]; le cirque est la représentation qui me semble la plus tragique. A travers les siècles, c'est le cri le plus aigu dans la recherche de l'amusement et la joie de l'homme. Il prend souvent la forme de la haute poésie. »

Toutes ses tapisseries furent réalisées d'après des œuvres que l'artiste avait peintes dans ses années de maturité. Chagall fut très heureux de la première tapisserie qu'Yvette Cauquil-Prince effectua sur le thème du cirque. Ce fut le début d'une collaboration qui allait durer vingt ans et donner au total 29 tapisseries de tailles diverses, dont certaines très grandes. Daniel Alcouffe, conservateur au Louvre, parla de « l'admiration que suscite son œuvre... Elle est heureuse de pouvoir remplir sa tâche et rayonne d'une profonde sérénité ». Bella Meyer, la petite-fille de Chagall, voyait dans l'œuvre d'Yvette

Paul Klee
Actor, 1971
Schauspieler
Acteur

Tapestry, manufactured by master-craftswoman Yvette Cauquil-Prince after the work on paper "Schauspieler", 1923–1927 (Private collection, Switzerland)
165 x 95 cm
Private collection

Pablo Picasso
La Minotauromachie, 1991

Tapestry, manufactured by master-
craftswoman Yvette Cauquil-Prince
after the etching "La Minotauromachie",
1935 (Musée Picasso, Paris)
315 x 450 cm
Private collection, Paris
© Succession Picasso/
VG Bild-Kunst, Bonn 1999

Pablo Picasso
Farmer's Wife (Woman with Doves), 1965
Die Bäuerin (Frau mit Tauben)
La Fermière (Femme aux pigeons)

Tapestry, manufactured by master-crafts-
woman Yvette Cauquil-Prince after the
painting "La Femme aux pigeons", 1930
(Musée national d'art moderne, Paris)
213 x 178 cm
Antibes (France), Musée Picasso
© Succession Picasso/
VG Bild-Kunst, Bonn 1999

In the course of her long career, Mme. Cauquil-Prince has produced more than 80 tapestries for leading artists of the twentieth century. The tapestries she created for Marc Chagall cover the whole spectrum of his themes: the Bible and the prophets, the circus, life, flowers, dancing, peace. Through her skill and professionalism, Yvette Cauquil-Prince could transform a gouache or watercolour painting into a new, large-scale artwork without losing the essence and character of the original or deviating from the intention of the artist. Each of her tapestries is infused with a love of and respect for the original work. In dialogue with her various 'client' artists, and with the greatest devotion and patience, she has during her long career upheld the age-old traditions of tapestry weaving, bringing the craft in the 20th century to new heights.

dessen Spiel der Beine und Arme die Formen großer Kunst annehmen. [...] Der Zirkus ist für mich die tragischste Darstellung. Durch die Jahrhunderte der durchdringendste Schrei auf der Suche nach dem Vergnügen und der Freude des Menschen. Er nimmt oft die Form großer Poesie an.«

Alle Tapisserien von Chagall sind nach Gemälden seines Spätwerks entstanden. Mit diesem ersten Teppich von Yvette Cauquil-Prince war der Künstler überaus zufrieden. Dieses Werk stand am Beginn einer zwanzigjährigen Zusammenarbeit, aus der 29 Chagall-Tapisserien in unterschiedlichen, zum Teil sehr großen Formaten, hervorgingen. Daniel Alcouffe, Kurator im Louvre, sprach von »der Bewunderung, die ihr Werk auslöst. [...] Sie ist glücklich, ihre eigene Aufgabe erfüllen zu können, und strahlt eine tiefe innere Ruhe aus.« Bella Meyer, Chagalls Enkelin, sieht in dem Werk von Cauquil-Prince »eine artikulierte Sprache, unmittelbar, offen und klar. Sie erhebt sich wie die Erinnerung an einen Mythos.«

In ihrer langen Laufbahn hat Yvette Cauquil-Prince mehr als 80 Tapisserien für bedeutende Künstler unseres Jahrhunderts geschaffen. Die für Marc Chagall gefertigten Teppiche führen die ganze Bandbreite seiner Themen vor Augen: die Bibel und ihre Propheten, der Zirkus, das Leben, Blumen, der Tanz und der Frieden. Dank ihrer Kunstfertigkeit und Professionalität vermochte es Yvette Cauquil-Prince, eine Gouache oder ein Aquarell in ein neues, großformatiges Kunstwerk zu transformieren, ohne daß dabei das Wesen der Vorlage, die ursprüngliche Intention des Künstlers verlorengegangen wäre. In jede ihrer Tapisserien ist nicht nur ihre technische Meisterschaft, sondern auch ein Übermaß an Liebe und Respekt für das Originalwerk des Künstlers eingegangen. Im Dialog mit den verschiedenen Künstlern und mit größter Hingabe und Geduld hat sie im Laufe ihrer langen Karriere die alte Kunst der Bildweberei im 20. Jahrhundert zu einer neuen Blüte geführt.

Cauquil-Prince un « langage articulé, franc et clair, émergeant comme la réminiscence d'un mythe ».

Durant sa longue carrière, Yvette Cauquil-Prince a réalisé plus de 80 tapisseries pour les plus grands artistes de notre siècle. Les tapisseries effectuées pour Marc Chagall montrent les motifs les plus divers de l'artiste – la Bible et les prophètes, le cirque, la vie, les fleurs, la danse et la paix. Grâce à son habileté et à la très grande perfection de son travail, Yvette Cauquil-Prince sut transformer une gouache ou une aquarelle en une création nouvelle, sans perdre l'essence, le caractère et l'intention de l'artiste. Chacune de ses tapisseries révèle non seulement toute sa maîtrise technique mais aussi une profonde vénération pour l'œuvre originale. Dans son dialogue avec les artistes les plus divers et par son infinie patience, elle permit à l'art traditionnel de la tapisserie de connaître au XXe siècle un nouvel épanouissement.

TOP/OBEN/EN HAUT
Yvette Cauquil-Prince in front of her Chagall tapestry "Moses", 1993
Yvette Cauquil-Prince vor ihrer Chagall-Tapisserie »Moses«
Yvette Cauquil-Prince devant la tapisserie de Chagall « Moïse »

BOTTOM/UNTEN/EN BAS
Yvette Cauquil-Prince weaving a Chagall tapestry
Yvette Cauquil-Prince beim Weben einer Chagall-Tapisserie
Yvette Cauquil-Prince tissant une des tapisseries de Chagall

The Entry into Jerusalem, 1963–1964
Der Einzug in Jerusalem
L'Entrée à Jérusalem

Tapestry manufactured at the Manufacture
nationale des Gobelins in Paris by master-
craftsman M. Bourbonneaux
475 x 528 cm
Jerusalem, The Knesset

Chagall Marc 1964

Tapestry, manufactured at the Manufacture
nationale des Gobelins in Paris by master-
craftsman M. E. Lelong
475 x 904 cm
Jerusalem, The Knesset

Isaiah's Prophecy, 1964–1967
Die Prophezeiung Jesajas
La Prophétie d'Isaïe

Tapestry, manufactured at the Manufacture
nationale des Gobelins in Paris by master-
craftsman M. E. Meot
475 x 533 cm
Jerusalem, The Knesset
Photo: Werner Braun, Jerusalem

Exodus (detail), 1963
Exodus (Detail)
L'Exode (détail)

Exodus (detail), 1963
Exodus (Detail)
L'Exode (détail)

Isaiah's Prophecy (detail), 1963
Die Prophezeiung Jesajas (Detail)
La Prophétie d'Isaïe (détail)

Gouache and drawing
126.7 x 144.5 cm
Private collection

Isaiah's Prophecy (detail), 1963
Die Prophezeiung Jesajas (Detail)
La Prophétie d'Isaïe (détail)

Gouache and drawing
126.7 x 144.5 cm
Private collection

"For me, a circus is a magic show that appears and disappears like a world. There is a disquieting circus, and a true one. [...] The clowns, the riders, the acrobats have taken root in my visions. Why do their get-up and their grimaces move me? With them I approach other horizons. The circus seems to me to be the most tragic show on earth, man's most poignant cry across the centuries in his search for amusement and joy. It often takes the form of high poetry."

»Für mich ist der Zirkus ein magisches Schauspiel, das kommt und vergeht wie eine Welt. Es gibt einen beunruhigenden Zirkus, einen wahren. [...] Die Clowns, die Reiter, die Akrobaten haben sich in meinen Visionen festgesetzt. Warum berühren mich ihre Aufmachung und ihre Grimassen? Mit ihnen nähere ich mich anderen Horizonten. Der Zirkus ist für mich die tragischste Darstellung. Durch die Jahrhunderte der durchdringendste Schrei auf der Suche nach dem Vergnügen und der Freude des Menschen. Er nimmt oft die Form großer Poesie an.«

« Pour moi un cirque est un spectacle magique qui passe et fond comme un monde. Il y a un cirque inquiétant, un cirque profond. Ces clowns, ces écuyères, ces acrobates se sont installés dans mes visions. Pourquoi leurs maquillages et leurs grimaces m'émeuvent-ils ? Je m'approche avec eux d'autres horizons ; le cirque est la représentation qui me semble la plus tragique. A travers les siècles, c'est le cri le plus aigu dans la recherche de l'amusement et la joie de l'homme. Il prend souvent la forme de la haute poésie. ».

Marc Chagall

Circus I, 1966
Zirkus I
Cirque I

Tapestry, manufactured by master-craftswoman Yvette Cauquil-Prince
282 x 190 cm
Heidelberg, Textilmuseum Max Berk
Photo: Claude Gaspari

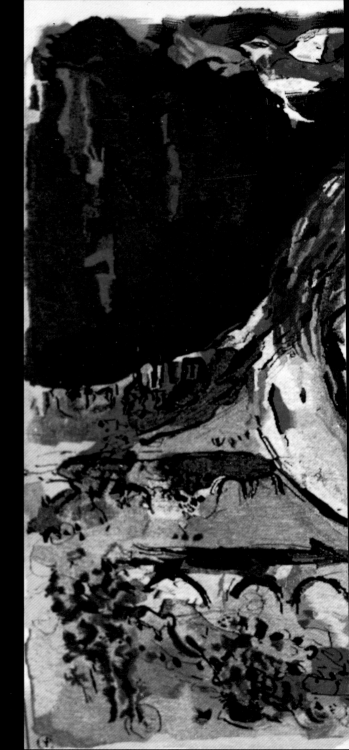

The Blue Night, 1969
Die blaue Nacht
La Nuit bleue

Tapestry, manufactured by master-craftswoman Yvette Cauquil-Prince
206 x 270 cm
Private collection
Photo: Claude Gaspari

The weaving of tapestries is like a ceremonial act. It is a song, a song of epic solemnity: a polyphonic choir, in which the singers (the weavers), [...] as befits performing artists, must needs keep their eyes fixed on the conductor's baton. The conductor himself though (who, in my mind, belongs to the family of creative artists), responding to his innermost calling, must construct the piece, direct it, give it meaning, bring out the finest details."

»Das Weben von Wandteppichen ist eine feierliche Handlung. Es ist ein Gesang, ein Gesang von epischer Getragenheit: ein vielstimmiger Chor, dessen Sänger (die Weber) [...] beim Singen die Augen unablässig auf den Dirigentenstab richten müssen. Der Dirigent aber, den ich zur Familie der schöpferischen Künstler zähle, ist seiner innersten Bestimmung nach dazu ausersehen, das Stück aufzubauen, es zu leiten, ihm Ausdruck zu verleihen, Feinheiten hervorzuheben.«

« La tapisserie murale est chose grave. C'est un chant : et, qui plus est, un chant d'intentions épiques : un chœur à plusieurs voix dont les participants (les lissiers) doivent, [...] comme il sied à tout exécutant, pousser leur voix les yeux fixés sur le bâton du chef d'orchestre. Chef, je l'entends donc sous les espèces de l'artiste ; c'est-à-dire un homme qui par destination et fatalité est fait pour construire puis diriger le morceau, commander à l'expression, souligner certaines nuances. »

Jean Lurçat

The Dance (The Opera), 1969
Der Tanz (Die Oper)
La Danse (l'Opéra)

Tapestry, manufactured by master-craftswoman Yvette Cauquil-Prince
after the lithograph "L'Opéra", 1954
270 x 130 cm
Private collection

Marc Chagall

"I have always thought of clowns, acrobats and actors as tragically human beings, who for me resemble the figures in certain religious paintings."

»Ich habe Clowns, Akrobaten und Schauspieler immer als auf tragische Weise menschliche Wesen betrachtet, die für mich den Personen auf gewissen religiösen Gemälden gleichen.«

« J'ai toujours considéré les clowns, les acrobates et les acteurs comme des êtres tragiquement humains, qui ressemblent, pour moi, aux personnages de certains tableaux religieux. »

Marc Chagall

The Harlequin Family, 1970
Die Harlekinfamilie
La Famille d'Arlequin

Tapestry, manufactured by master-craftswoman Yvette Cauquil-Prince after
the lithograph "La Famille d'Arlequin"
(1964–1965)
205 x 155 cm
Private collection
Photo: Courtesy Jane Kahan Gallery,
New York

"In the beginning God created the heaven and the earth [...] And God said, Let there be light: and there was light [...] And God said, Let the earth bring forth the living creature after his kind, cattle, and creeping thing, and beast of the earth after his kind. And God made the beast of the earth after his kind, and cattle after their kind, and every thing that creepeth upon the earth after his kind... And God said, Let us make man in our image, after our likeness : and let them have dominion over the fish of the sea, and over the fowl of the air, and over the cattle, and over all the earth, and over every creeping thing that creepeth upon the earth."

»Im Anfang schuf Gott Himmel und Erde [...] Gott sprach: Es werde Licht. Und es wurde Licht [...] Dann sprach Gott: Das Land bringe alle Arten von lebendigen Wesen hervor, von Vieh, von Kriechtieren und von Tieren des Feldes [...] Dann sprach Gott: Laßt uns Menschen machen als unser Abbild, uns ähnlich. Sie sollen herrschen über die Fische des Meeres, über die Vögel des Himmels, über das Vieh, über die ganze Erde und über alle Kriechtiere auf dem Land.«

« Au commencement, Dieu créa le ciel et la terre [...] » Dieu dit: « Que la lumière soit » et la lumière fut [...] Dieu dit : « Que la terre produise des êtres vivants selon leur espèce : bestiaux, bestioles, bêtes sauvages selon leur espèce ». [...] Dieu dit : « Faisons l'homme à notre image, comme notre ressemblance, et qu'ils dominent sur les poissons de la mer, les oiseaux du ciel, les bestiaux, toutes les bêtes sauvages et toutes les bestioles qui rampent sur la terre. »

Genesis 1,1; 1,3; 1,24; 1,26

The Creation, 1971
Die Schöpfung
La Création

Tapestry, manufactured by master-crafts-woman Yvette Cauquil-Prince after the gouache "La Création", 1956–1959
256 x 186 cm
Private collection
Photo: Claude Gaspari

"One must quench the richness of colour with one's
soul."

»Man muß den Reichtum der Farbe mit der Seele
löschen!«

« Il faut tuer la richesse de la couleur avec le psychique. »
Marc Chagall

"Colour and line contain the artist's whole character and
message."

»In den Farben und den Linien ist der Charakter und die
Botschaft des Künstlers enthalten.«

« Dans les couleurs et les lignes sont contenus le caractère
et le message de l'artiste. »
Marc Chagall

"A painter does not usually have a true picture of himself.
But he may achieve this with time. In old age you look
back over your life. You see through yourself, as if from
outside, and paint your inner life as if you were painting
a still life."

»Im allgemeinen bekommt ein Maler sich selbst nicht in
den Blick. Aber vielleicht gelingt ihm das im Alter. Im
Alter überblickt man sein Leben. Man sieht in sich hin-
ein, wie von außen, und man malt sein Innenleben so
als würde man ein Stilleben malen.«

« En général, l'artiste ne peut pas se voir. Mais peut-être
l'âge lui en donne la permission. Avec l'âge, on voit soi-
même sa vie. On regarde en dedans de soi comme si
c'était dehors, on peint son intérieur comme une nature
morte. »

Marc Chagall

Composition in Blue , 1972
Komposition in Blau
Composition en bleu

Tapestry, manufactured by master-craftswoman Yvette Cauquil-Prince after the
lithograph "Nocturne", 1964–1965
230 x 175 cm
Private collection

"It is not for me to talk about myself and my work. My aim was to get closer to the biblical homeland of the Jewish people, to the land where the creative spirit, the Holy Spirit, is at home, such as hovers over every page of the Bible and hovers here in the air, over the fields, and in the hearts and souls of the inhabitants."

»Es ist nicht meine Aufgabe, über mich selbst und mein Werk zu sprechen. Mein Ziel war es, mich der angestammten biblischen Heimat des jüdischen Volkes anzunähern, dem Land, wo der Schöpfergeist zu finden ist, der sich auf jeder Seite der Bibel findet. Er schwebt in der Luft, über den Feldern und in den Herzen und Seelen der Menschen, die das Land bewohnen.«

« Ce n'est pas à moi de parler de moi-même et de mon œuvre. Mon but était de me rapprocher de la patrie biblique du peuple juif, de la terre où se trouve l'esprit créateur que l'on trouve dans chaque page de la Bible et qui est ici, flottant dans l'air, au-dessus des champs et dans le cœur et l'âme des habitants. »

Marc Chagall

Moses, 1973
Moses
Moïse

Tapestry, manufactured by master-craftswoman Yvette Cauquil-Prince after the lithograph "Composition", 1964–1965
320 x 233 cm
Private collection
Photo: Claude Gaspari

The Prophet Jeremiah

"The image of the prophet tells of the history of the chosen people of God and in the pages are written the prophecies of peace, of wisdom, and of the understanding between all the peoples of the earth for the future. The red bird symbolises joy and hope and seems to sing the Song of Songs.

The red colour of the bird makes an illusion to the long sufferings of the Jewish people across the centuries, their sacrifices and their innocence.

In painting the woman, I thought of the women of the Bible, of Madame Golda Meir, and of all the valiant women of the earth. In depicting the other women, my thoughts went to Madame Helfaer.

The blue represents the colour of hope and of the new Israel.

The blue colour of the other bird, symbolises the hope of life, of truth, and of good fortune for all of humanity. The moon, in another era in my life, permitted me to dream of a better future."

Der Prophet Jeremia

»Die Darstellung des Propheten erzählt von der Geschichte des auserwählten Volkes Gottes, und auf den Seiten sind die Verheißungen des Friedens, der Weisheit und der Verständigung zwischen allen Völkern der Erde niedergeschrieben. Der rote Vogel symbolisiert die Freude und die Hoffnung; er scheint das Lied der Lieder zu singen. Die rote Farbe des Vogels spielt auf die Leidensgeschichte des jüdischen Volkes an, die Jahrhunderte des Exils und der Wanderschaft, auf die Opferbereitschaft und die Unschuld dieses Volkes. Als ich die Frau malte, standen die Frauen der Bibel vor meinem inneren Auge, Madame Golda Meir und alle tapferen Frauen dieser Welt. In die Darstellung der anderen Frauen sind meine Gedanken an Madame Helfaer eingegangen. Das Blau repräsentiert die Farbe der Hoffnung und des neuen Israel. Die blaue Farbe des anderen Vogels symbolisiert die Hoffnung auf Leben, auf Wahrheit und auf eine glückliche Zukunft für die ganze Menschheit. Der Mond stand in einem früheren Abschnitt meines Lebens für den Traum der Menschen von einer besseren Zukunft.«

Le Prophète Jérémie

« L'image du prophète illustre l'histoire du peuple élu de Dieu ; dans ces pages sont écrites les prophéties de Paix, de Sagesse et la compréhension pour l'avenir entre tous les peuples de la terre.
L'oiseau rouge symbolise la joie et l'espoir et il semble chanter le Cantique des Cantiques. La couleur rouge de l'oiseau fait allusion aux longues souffrances du peuple juif à travers les siècles, à ses sacrifices et à son innocence. En peignant la femme, j'ai pensé aux femmes de la Bible, à Madame Golda Meir et à toutes les femmes courageuses de la terre. En peignant les autres femmes, mes pensées allaient à Madame Helfaer. Le bleu représente la couleur de l'espoir et d'un nouvel Israël. L'autre oiseau, le bleu, symbolise l'espoir de vie, de vérité et de bonheur pour toute l'humanité. La lune, dans une autre phase de ma vie, nous a permis de rêver à un avenir meilleur. »

"The drawing of this tapestry has been made by me at the request of Mr Albert Adelman, intermediary for Mr Helfaer.

I have interpreted the meaning of the tapestry for Evan and Marion Helfaer."

Marc Chagall

»Der Karton für diese Tapisserie wurde von mir für Mr. Helfaer ausgeführt, der mich über Mr. Albert Adelman um dieses Werk gebeten hatte.

Diese Deutung meines Bildteppichs ist Evan und Marion Helfaer zugeeignet.«

Marc Chagall

« Le dessin de la tapisserie a été fait par moi sur la demande de M. Albert Adelmann, l'intermédiaire de M. Helfaer.

J'ai interprété le sens de la tapisserie pour Evan et Marion Helfaer. »

Marc Chagall

The Prophet Jeremiah, 1973
Der Prophet Jeremia
Le Prophète Jérémie

Tapestry (unique piece), manufactured by
master-craftswoman Yvette Cauquil-Prince
after the gouache "Le Prophète" (Dessin
pour la Bible), no date (1958–1959)
400 x 600 cm
Milwaukee (WI), Jewish Federation Center

Marc Chagall

"If ever there was a moral crisis, it is that of paint, matter, blood, and all their constituents – the words and tones, all the things out of which one makes a life or creates art. For even if you cover a canvas with thick masses of paint, irrespective of whether the outlines of shapes can be made out or not, and even if you enlist the help of words and sounds, it does not necessarily follow that an authentic work of art will emerge."

»Wenn es je eine moralische Krise gab, so die der Farbe, der Materie, des Blutes und ihrer Elemente, der Worte und Töne, all jener Dinge, aus denen man ein Kunstwerk erschafft wie auch ein Leben. Denn selbst wenn man eine Leinwand mit Wülsten von Farbe bedeckt, gleich-viel, ob dabei Umrisse zu erkennen sind oder nicht – und selbst wenn man Wort und Töne zu Hilfe nimmt –, so entsteht deshalb nicht unbedingt ein authentisches Kunstwerk.«

« S'il y a jamais eu une crise morale, ce fut bien celle de la couleur, de la matière, du sang et de tous leurs consti-tuants, les mots et les sons, toutes ces choses à partir desquelles on crée une œuvre d'art comme on crée une vie. Car même si vous couvrez une toile avec d'épaisses couches de peinture, que l'on reconnaisse ou non les contours, et que vous faites appel aux mots et aux sons, vous n'aurez pas nécessairement créé une œuvre d'art authentique. »

Marc Chagall

PAGE/SEITE /PAGE 54/55
David and Bathsheba, 1973
David und Batseba
David et Bethsabée

Tapestry, manufactured by master-crafts-woman Yvette Cauquil-Prince after a watercolor for the VERVE Bible II, 1960
247 x 404 cm
Private collection

Profile in Blue and Yellow, 1973
Profil in Blau und Gelb
Profil en bleu et jaune

Tapestry, manufactured by master-crafts-woman Yvette Cauquil-Prince after the monotype which served as the poster for the exhibition "Chagall, peintures 1947–1967" at the Fondation Maeght, Saint-Paul-de-Vence, 1967
181 x 133 cm
Private collection
Photo: Claude Germain

Tapestry for the entrance hall of the
Musée National Message Biblique
Marc Chagall, Nice, c. 1974
Tapisserie für die Eingangshalle des
Musée National Message Biblique
Marc Chagall in Nizza
Tapisserie pour l'entrée du Musée
National Message Biblique Marc
Chagall, Nice

Wool, manufactured at the Manufacture
nationale des Gobelins, Paris
226 x 322 cm
Nice, Musée National Message Biblique
Marc Chagall
Photo: Gérard Blot

The Painter's Dream
Der Traum des Künstlers
Le Rêve du peintre

Tapestry, manufactured by master-
crafts- woman Yvette Cauquil-Prince
after the lithograph "Le Bouquet du
peintre",
1973

Song of Songs, 197
Das Lied der Lieder (Das Hohelied Salomos
Le Cantique des Cantiq

Marc Chagall

Circus II (detail), 1974–1975
Zirkus II (Detail)
Cirque II (détail)

Tapestry, manufactured by master-
craftswoman Yvette Cauquil-Prince
275 x 192 cm
Private collection

Circus II (detail), 1974–1975
Zirkus II (Detail)
Cirque II (détail)

Tapestry, manufactured by master-craftswoman Yvette Cauquil-Prince
275 x 192 cm
Private collection

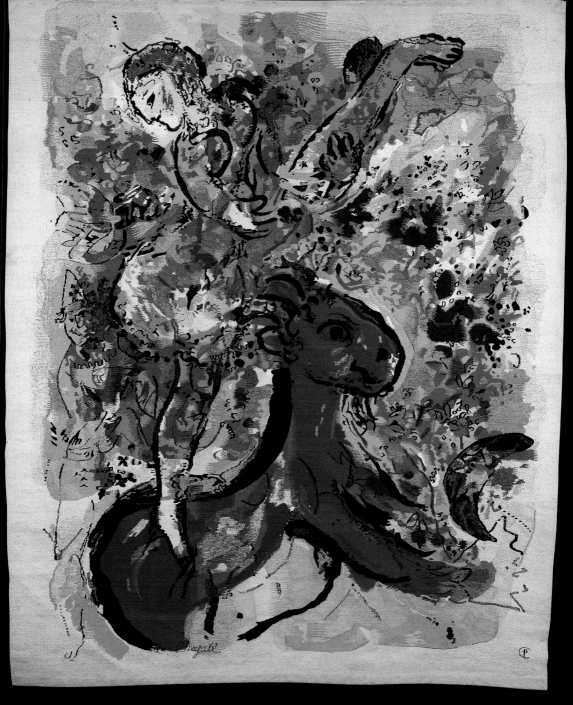

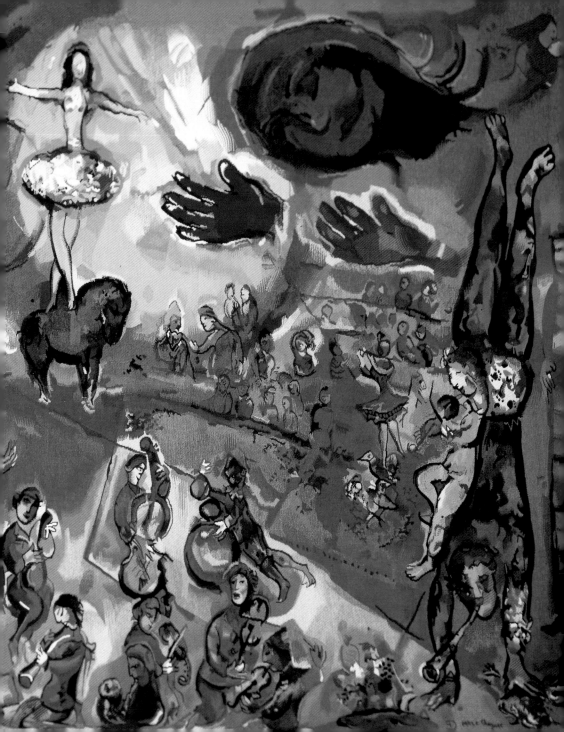

"For me, fulfilment in art and in life comes from this biblical source. Without this spirit, the mechanics of logic
and constructivism in art, as in life, cannot bear fruit."

» Für mich entspringt die Vollkommenheit in der Kunst
und im Leben aus dieser biblischen Quelle. Die Mechanik
der Logik und Konstruktivität allein bringt in der Kunst
wie im Leben ohne diesen Geist keine Frucht. «

« Pour moi, la perfection dans l'art et dans la vie provient
de cette source biblique. Sans cet esprit, les mécanismes
de logique et de constructivisme ne peuvent porter de
fruits. »

Marc Chagall

Life, 1989
Das Leben
La Vie

Tapestry (unique piece), manufactured by
master-craftswoman Yvette Cauquil-Prince
361 x 485 cm
Private collection
Photo: Claude Gaspari

The Event, 1990
Das Ereignis
L'Événement

Tapestry (unique piece), manufactured by
master-craftswoman Yvette Cauquil-Prince
293 x 355 cm
Private collection
Photo: Claude Gaspari

"The material from which tapestries are made is warmer and more costly than that of wall paintings. They reflect the joy in rare and exquisite things, executed with patient love and care, that is a defining feature of this culture."

» Das Material, aus dem Bildteppiche gearbeitet sind, ist wärmer und kostbarer als das der Wandmalerei. Sie spiegeln die Freude am Seltenen, Erlesenen, mit Liebe und Bedacht Ausgeführten, die das eigentliche Wesen dieser Kultur ausmacht. «

« Plus que la matière murale, la matière dont elle [la tapis-serie] est faite est chaude et subtile. Elle satisfait ce goût de la chose rare, précieuse, lentement travaillée, qui est au cœur de cette civilisation, et en même temps elle la maintient dans l'ordre des vraies grandeurs. »

Henri Focillon

Animal Tales, 1991
Tiererzählungen
Le Bestiaire

Tapestry (unique piece), manufactured by master-craftswoman Yvette Cauquil-Prince after the painting "Animals and Music", 1969
420 x 435 cm
Private collection
Photo: Claude Gaspari

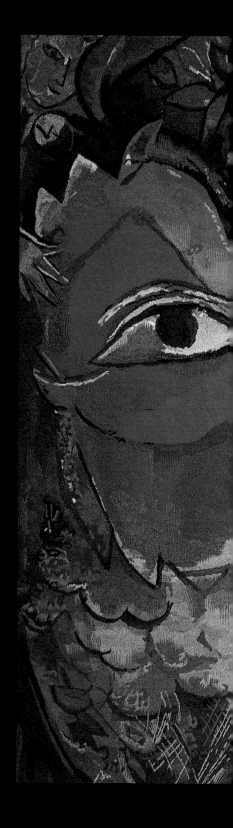

"The habit of ignoring nature is deeply implanted in our times. This attitude reminds me of people who never look you in the eye: I find them disturbing and always have to look away."

»Es ist in unsern Tagen so eingerissen, die Natur zu ignorieren. Diese Haltung erinnert mich an jene Menschen, die einem niemals ins Auge sehen; sie sind mir unheimlich, und ich muß immer wegschauen.«

« C'est devenu aujourd'hui une habitude d'ignorer la nature. Cette attitude me rappelle les gens qui ne vous regardent jamais dans les yeux ; je trouve cela désagréable et je regarde toujours ailleurs. »

Marc Chagall

The Red Rooster, 1991
Der rote Hahn
Le Coq rouge

Tapestry (unique piece), manufactured by master-craftswoman Yvette Cauquil-Prince after the painting "The Rooster in Love (Le Coq amoureux)", 1947–1950
315 x 380 cm
Private collection
Photo: Claude Germain

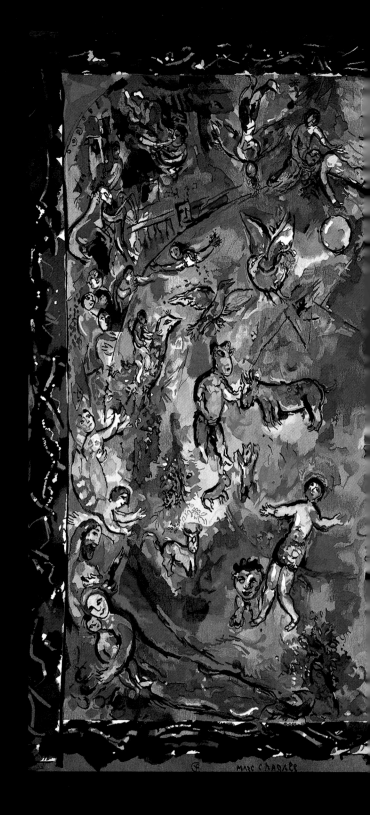

Peace, 1993
Der Friede
La Paix

Tapestry, manufactured by master-crafts-
woman Yvette Cauquil-Prince after the
stained-glass-window "Peace", 1964
(New York, The United Nations)
328 x 470 cm
Sarrebourg (France), Collection of the
Chapelle des Cordeliers
Photo: Claude Gaspari

76

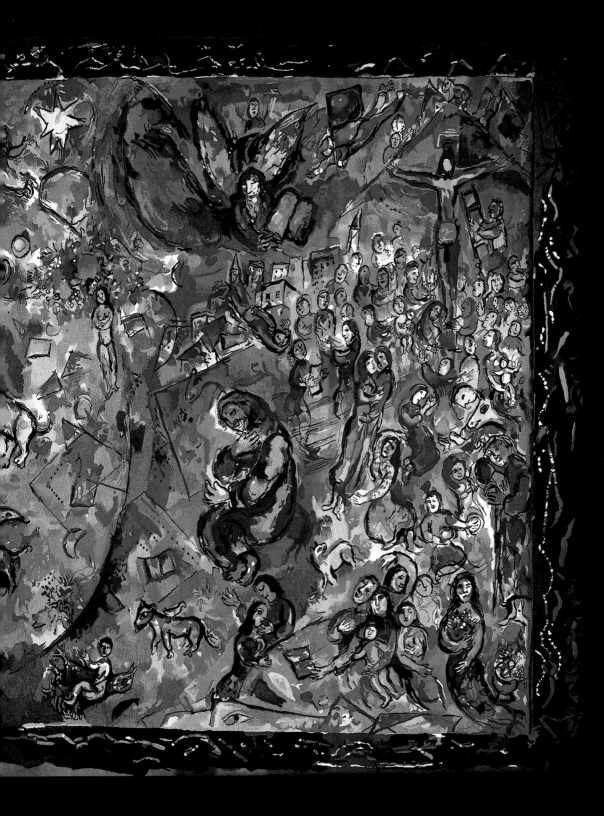

"Our whole inner world is reality – perhaps even more
real than the visible world."

»Unsere ganze innere Welt ist Wirklichkeit – vielleicht
sogar wirklicher als die sichtbare Welt.«

« Tout notre monde intérieur est réel – peut-être même
plus réel que le monde visible. »

Marc Chagall

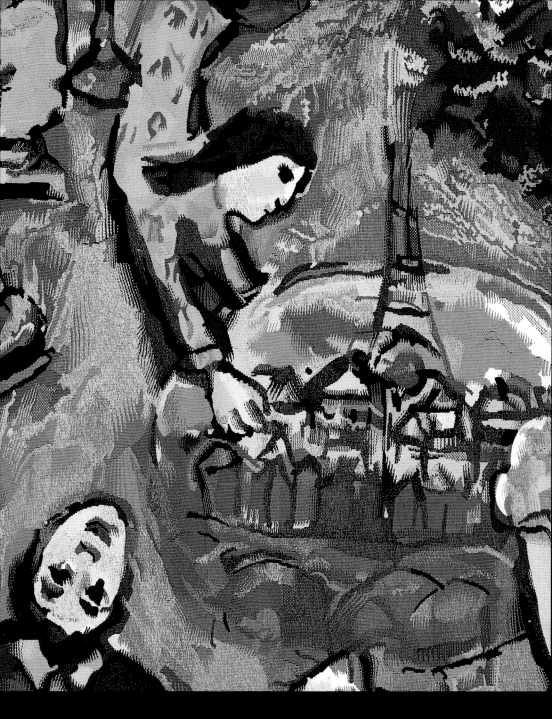

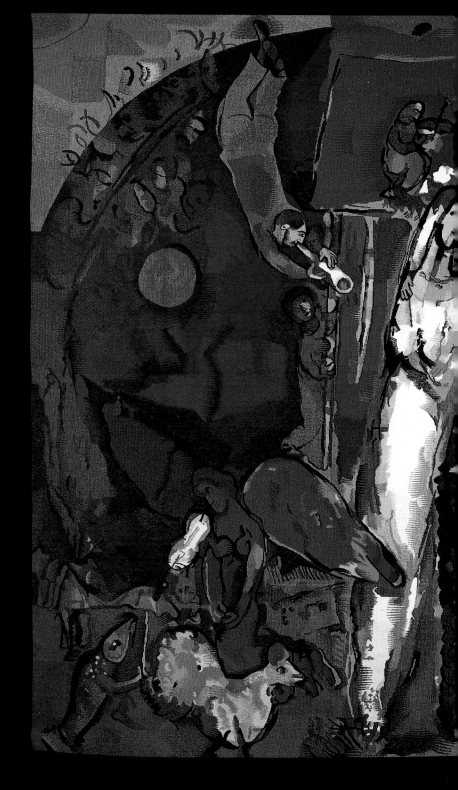

To My Wife, 1994
An meine Frau
À ma Femme

Tapestry (unique piece),
manufactured by
master-craftswoman
Yvette Cauquil-Prince
after the Painting "To
My Wife (À ma Femme)",
1933–1944
230 x 175 cm
Private collection
Photo: Claude Gaspari

"When Chagall paints, you do not know if he is asleep or awake. Somewhere or other inside his head there must be an angel."

» Wenn Chagall malt, weiß man nicht, ob er dabei schläft oder wach ist. Irgendwo in seinem Kopf muß er einen Engel haben. «

« Quand Chagall peint, on ne sait pas s'il dort ou s'il est éveillé. Un ange se trouve certainement quelque part dans sa tête. »

Pablo Picasso

"When I work from my heart, almost everything comes right, but when from my head, almost nothing."

» Wenn ich vom Herzen aus arbeite, gelingt fast alles, wenn ich vom Kopf aus arbeite, gelingt dagegen fast nichts. «

« Lorsque je travaille avec mon cœur, tout fonctionne ; si c'est avec ma tête, presque rien. »

Marc Chagall

The Dance, 1997
Der Tanz
La Danse

Tapestry, manufactured by master-crafts-woman Yvette Cauquil-Prince after the painting "The Dance (La Danse)", 1950 (Paris, Musée national d'art moderne, Centre Georges Pompidou)
261 x 200 cm
Private collection, Japan
Photo: Musée des Beaux-Arts de la Ville de Mons, Belgium

84

"The true validity of a work of art is demonstrated when it is translated into a tapestry. Its enlarged projection proves its physical existence, while magnifying it to startling proportions denies neither the artwork's material nor spiritual form [...] By placing herself at the service of artists, [...] Mme Cauquil-Prince has chosen to forget herself and to paint through weaving. She derives satisfaction from an unexpected intimacy, a marvellous state of grace in which she brings to life again the gifts entrusted to her by the artists who have chosen her, or whom she has chosen."

François Mathey
Former chief curator of the Musée des Arts Décoratifs, Paris

»Die wahre Gültigkeit eines Kunstwerks erweist sich, wenn es in einen Bildteppich umgesetzt wird; seine Vergrößerung beweist seine physische Existenz, selbst die Ausdehnung in verblüffende Dimensionen leugnet die materielle oder spirituelle Form des Kunstwerks nicht. [...] Indem sie sich selbst in den Dienst der Künstler stellt, [...] hat Mme. Cauquil-Prince sich dazu entschlossen, sich selbst hintan zu stellen und zu malen, indem sie webt. Ihre Befriedigung gewinnt sie aus einer unerwarteten Intimität, einem wunderbaren Zustand der Gnade, indem sie die Gaben erneut zum Leben erweckt, die ihr die Künstler, die sich für sie entschieden haben oder für die sie sich entschieden hat, anvertraut haben.«

François Mathey
Ehemaliger Chefkurator des Musée des Arts Décoratifs, Paris

« Ainsi reportée sur une tapisserie, l'œuvre d'art démontre sa véritable validité ; par extension, elle prouve son existence physique. Lui donner des dimensions aussi étonnantes n'enlève rien à sa forme matérielle ou spirituelle. [...] En se mettant ainsi au service des artistes, en leur offrant tout son travail et sa patience, [...] Madame Cauquil-Prince, a choisi de se mettre elle-même en retrait et de peindre en tissant. Elle tire sa satisfaction d'une intimité inattendue, un merveilleux état de grâce, dans lequel elle fait renaître les dons que les artistes qui l'ont choisie, ou qu'elle a choisis, lui ont confiés... »

François Mathey
Ancien conservateur en chef du Musée des Arts décoratifs, Paris

The Big Circus (detail), 1985
Der große Zirkus (Detail)
Le Grand Cirque (détail)

Tapestry (unique piece), manufactured
by master-craftswoman Yvette
Cauquil-Prince
c. 300 x 600 cm
Private collection
Photo: Claude Gaspari

Marc Chagall with Yvette Cauquil-Prince, c. 1966
Marc Chagall mit Yvette Cauquil-Prince, ca. 1966
Marc Chagall avec Yvette Cauquil-Prince, vers 1966

Yvette Cauquil-Prince
The Tapestries of Marc Chagall

The beginning of my work on the tapestries of Marc Chagall coincided with the last stages of the production of his wall hangings for the Knesset by the Manufacture nationale des Gobelins in Paris. The translation of Chagall's gouaches into tapestries proved problematic in many ways.

For me it was a stroke of luck to be drawn into this venture, which demanded not only great precision and respect, but also love and intuition, as I was drawn ever closer to Chagall's work. It was the beginning of a collaboration that has continued to this day.

After intensive studies at the Ecole des Beaux-Arts in Belgium, I devoted myself to painting, although for many years I had been especially interested in tapestries from the 15th, 16th and 17th centuries, as well as in some works from the 18th century. My first encounter with Coptic works, passed down to us from the first and second centuries AD, awakened in me a passion for this art form, while the tapestries of the 19th and 20th centuries held little appeal, and seemed to me, with a few exceptions, very poor in comparison. Even the tapestries of Goya pale beside any one of that master's engravings or paintings.

And the Copts had indeed discovered everything that was later to be found in the European tradition of tapestry weaving: the stretching of the fabric in a frame, hatching, shading and selecting weft threads of varying strengths to match the particular demands of the original picture. My task as a weaver was to place the full potential of this technique, as reached at its first zenith, at the service of leading artists of the present day.

My work with Marc Chagall was exemplary. The formal compositional elements to be found even in his most mysterious works, his lyricism and his poetry challenged me to use the full range of possibilities offered by this craft, whether the task in hand was the translation of a gouache, an oil painting or even a lithograph.

The most important and challenging aspect of the creation of a tapestry – regardless of who produced the cartoon – is that the new work must cover a far larger

Yvette Cauquil-Prince
Zu den Tapisserien von Marc Chagall

Yvette Cauquil-Prince
À propos des tapisseries de Marc Chagall

Der Beginn meiner Arbeit an den Tapisserien Marc Chagalls fällt mit der Herstellung seiner Wandteppiche für die Knesset durch die staatliche französische Gobelin-Manufaktur zusammen. Die Umsetzung der Gouachen von Chagall in Tapisserien erwies sich in mehrfacher Hinsicht als problematisch.

Für mich war dieses Abenteuer ein großer Glücksfall, und ich näherte mich dem Werk Chagalls mit großer Strenge und Respekt, aber ebenso mit Liebe und Intuition. Es war dies der Anfang einer Zusammenarbeit, die bis heute fortbesteht.

Nach intensivem Studium der Ecole des Beaux-Arts in Belgien widmete ich mich der Malerei, wobei mein besonderes Interesse jedoch seit meiner Jugendzeit alten Tapisserien aus dem 15., 16. und 17. Jahrhundert und einigen Werken des 18. Jahrhunderts galt. Die Begegnung mit den Arbeiten der Kopten aus den ersten Jahrhunderten n. Chr., die mich zum Staunen brachten, bestärkte mich in meiner Leidenschaft. Dem steht meine Ablehnung dem Werk des 19. und 20. Jahrhunderts gegenüber, das mir bis auf einige Ausnahmen völlig verarmt erscheint. Sogar die Tapisserien von Goya bestehen nicht neben einem Bild oder einem Stich dieses Meisters!

Tatsächlich haben bereits die Kopten alles entdeckt, was später in der europäischen Tradition der Tapisserien zu finden ist: das Gewebe in der Form, Schraffierungen, Abschattierungen, Schlußgarne verschiedener Stärke, abgestimmt auf die besonderen Erfordernisse des zu übertragenden Werkes. Meine Aufgabe war es daher, diese frühen Errungenschaften in den Dienst der Gegenwart zu stellen.

Meine Zusammenarbeit mit Marc Chagall war beispielhaft. Die Strenge, die im Geheimsten seines Werkes zu finden ist, seine Lyrik, seine Poesie erlaubten mir, die ganze Skala der Möglichkeiten des Metiers zu verwenden, ob es sich nun um die Übertragung einer Gouache, eines Ölbildes oder sogar einer Lithographie handelte.

Bei der Ausführung eines Bildteppichs ist – unabhängig vom Urheber der Vorlage – zuallererst zu bedenken, daß das neue Werk eine größere Wandfläche

Le début de mon travail sur les tapisseries de Marc Chagall coïncide avec la dernière partie de la fabrication de sa tapisserie réalisée pour la Knesseth par la Manufacture nationale des Gobelins. Transformer en tapisseries les gouaches de Chagall s'avéra problématique à plusieurs égards.

Ce fut pour moi une grande chance de pouvoir tenter cette aventure, qui me fit approcher l'œuvre de Chagall avec rigueur et respect, mais aussi avec sensibilité et amour. Ce fut le début d'un long travail en commun.

Après des études approfondies à l'École des beaux-arts en Belgique, je me suis consacrée à la peinture, alors que, depuis ma jeunesse, je m'intéressais tout particulièrement aux tapisseries anciennes des XVe, XVIe et XVIIe siècles et à quelques œuvres du XVIIIe siècle. La découverte, mêlant étonnement et enthousiasme, d'œuvres qui nous ont été transmises par les Coptes au début de notre ère, me conforta dans mon élan. En revanche, je n'avais aucune attirance pour les œuvres des XIXe et XXe siècles qui, à quelques exceptions près, me paraissaient totalement appauvries. Même les tapisseries de Goya ne peuvent tenir la comparaison avec une peinture ou une gravure de ce maître.

De fait, les Coptes avaient déjà tout découvert de ce que l'on trouvera plus tard dans la tradition européenne de la tapisserie : le tissu dans la forme, les hachures, les nuances, le fil de trame de différente épaisseur, selon l'exigence particulière de l'œuvre à transposer. Mon devoir était donc de mettre au service des maîtres contemporains les acquis d'une technique qui avait déjà connu un premier apogée.

Ma collaboration avec Marc Chagall fut à ce titre exemplaire. La rigueur, que l'on trouve au plus profond de son œuvre, son lyrisme, sa poésie m'ont permis d'utiliser toute la gamme des possibilités du métier, qu'il s'agisse de transposer une gouache, une peinture à l'huile ou même une lithographie.

Ce qui compte le plus dans la réalisation d'une tapisserie – indépendamment de l'auteur du modèle – c'est le fait que la nouvelle œuvre va occuper davantage

Drawing of a tapestry for the weavers
Vorzeichnung einer Tapisserie für die Teppichweber
Carton destiné aux tisserands

space on the wall, yet be conceived and visualised with great sensitivity and empathy for the original. Obviously, not all compositions are strong enough to survive this process of magnification from the comparative intimacy of a sheet of paper or a painting to the dimensions of a wall-covering design.

I was constantly filled with the spirit of Chagall's work and felt compelled to adhere faithfully to the intentions of the artist. Within the limits of my craft and in a format differing from that of the original, I had to strive to bring across his special intensity of colour and compositional formality, which amateurs so seldom perceive.

It was always immensely helpful to be able to discuss a tapestry with Chagall before its completion. We both agreed that unless the tapestries had achieved the full beauty and unique character of the original work they should be taken away and destroyed. Here, moments of joy and happiness alternated with periods of crushing insecurity, since no one is infallible. Yet under these circumstances, as Chagall said, I strove successfully for twenty years.

Today when, following Chagall's wishes, I devote most of my time to his monumental works, I very much miss his presence and the lively talks and laughter we shared. It has always given me great joy to find the hidden messages in his works and to be the mediator through whom they are passed on. Chagall felt I understood him and had the artistic talent to translate his art.

Now I must manage to carry on the work without that stimulating dialogue, supported by the trust of people that he loved and for whom I feel respect, empathy and gratefulness, friends who have made it possible for me to renew this pact of trust. With these few lines I would like to express my deep gratitude to the artist's widow, Valentina Chagall, and Madame Ida Chagall, the artist's daughter, and his generous and loving grandchildren Bella, Meret and Piet.

90

einnehmen wird, auf die man sich vorausblickend mit großem Einfühlungsvermögen einzustellen hat. Selbstverständlich verkraften nicht alle Kompositionen diesen Akt der Übertragung von der vergleichsweisen Intimität eines Blattes Papier oder eines Bildes in die Dimension einer wandfüllenden Gestaltung.

Immer fühlte ich mich dem Geist der Werke Chagalls und der Intention des Künstlers verpflichtet. Bedingt durch die andere Technik und das gegenüber der Vorlage andere Format galt es, die besondere Farbintensität und Formstrenge zu berücksichtigen, die für den Laien oft schwer zu begreifen ist.

Von größtem Wert erwies sich das Gespräch mit Chagall vor vollendeten Werken. Nach dem Willen des Meisters und nach meiner Vorstellung mußten die Tapisserien die ganze Schönheit und Eigenart der originalen Vorlage erreichen, um nicht zurückgezogen und vernichtet zu werden. Augenblicke des Glücks und der Freude wechselten hier oft mit Unsicherheit, denn schließlich ist niemand vor Fehlern gefeit; ein Umstand, dem ich mich, wie Chagall meinte, 20 Jahre hindurch erfolgreich widersetzen konnte.

Heute, wo ich dem Willen Chagalls entsprechend vor allem Monumentalwerken verpflichtet bin, fehlen mir seine Anwesenheit und das lebhafte, oftmals zum Lachen Anlaß gebende Gespräch mit ihm sehr. Für mich war es immer ein Glücksgefühl, die in seinen Werken verborgenen Absichten wahrnehmen und wiedergeben zu können. Chagall fühlte sich verstanden und künstlerisch in adäquater Weise umgesetzt.

Heute muß ich ohne diesen anregenden Dialog auskommen, unterstützt vom Vertrauen von Menschen, die ihm lieb waren und für die ich Respekt, Zuneigung und Dankbarkeit empfinde, da sie es mir ermöglicht haben, diesen Vertrauensakt zu erneuern. Ich möchte mit diesen bescheidenen Zeilen der verstorbenen Witwe des Künstlers, Valentina Chagall, sowie Ida Chagall, der Tochter des Künstlers, und seinen so aufgeschlossenen Enkeln Bella, Meret und Piet aufrichtig danken.

d'espace et qu'il faut pouvoir l'imaginer avec toute la sensibilité nécessaire. Bien entendu, toutes les compositions ne supportent pas cette transposition de l'intimité d'une feuille de papier ou d'un tableau à la dimension d'une création remplissant un mur entier.

Je me suis toujours fait une obligation de respecter l'esprit de l'œuvre de Chagall et l'intention de l'artiste. Étant donné la différence de technique et de format par rapport à l'original, il fallait tenir compte de l'exceptionnelle intensité des couleurs et de la rigueur formelle souvent très difficiles à saisir pour l'amateur.

Les échanges avec Chagall devant les œuvres achevées furent d'une très grande importance. Conformément à la volonté du maître, et selon ma propre conception, les tapisseries devaient acquérir toute la beauté et le caractère propres au modèle original, si l'on ne voulait pas qu'elles soient détruites. Des instants de bonheur et de joie alternaient avec des phases d'incertitude car, au fond, personne n'est à l'abri de l'erreur — d'après Chagall, j'ai pu surmonter cet obstacle avec succès pendant vingt ans.

Maintenant que, conformément à la volonté de Chagall, je m'occupe surtout d'œuvres monumentales, sa présence et nos vivants entretiens, qui étaient souvent aussi l'occasion de rire, me manquent beaucoup. Ce fut toujours pour moi un véritable bonheur que de percevoir et exprimer les intentions cachées dans ces œuvres. Chagall avait le sentiment que sa pensée était comprise et traduite artistiquement de façon adéquate.

Aujourd'hui, à défaut de ces dialogues stimulants, j'ai le soutien et la confiance de gens qui lui étaient chers et pour qui j'éprouve respect, affection et reconnaissance, car ils m'ont permis de renouveler ce pacte de confiance. Par ces quelques mots, je voudrais adresser mes remerciements les plus sincères à la veuve dícédée l'artiste, Valentina Chagall, à Ida Chagall, la fille de l'artiste, et à ses petits-enfants attentionnés, Bella, Meret et Piet.

Marc Chagall, 1908

Marc and Bella Chagall with their daughter Ida in their apartment in Paris (110, Avenue d'Orléans), 1024
Marc und Bella Chagall mit ihrer Tochter Ida in ihrer Wohnung in Paris (Nummer 110, Avenue d'Orléans)
Marc et Bella Chagall avec leur fille Ida dans leur appartement parisìen (au 110, avenue d'Orléans)

Biography

1887 Marc Chagall is born on 7 July as Moische Segal in Liosno near Vitebsk.

1906 Chagall enters the art school of the painter Yehuda Pen.

1907 Chagall is admitted to the painting school of the Imperial Society for the Promotion of the Arts.

1908 Chagall studies for some months at a private institution run by the painter Pavel Saidenberg.

1909 Chagall changes to the liberal Svanseva School. He meets Bella Rosenfeld, who six years later becomes his wife.

1910 Chagall attends the academies La Palette and La Grande Chaumière.

1911 Chagall moves to "La Ruche" (the beehive), a Parisian artists' colony.

1912 Chagall exhibits three pictures at the Salon des Indépendants.

1914 First one-man exhibition in the Berlin gallery "Der Sturm". Chagall travels from Berlin to Russia on a three-month visa, but is prevented from returning to Paris by the outbreak of the First World War.

1915 Chagall marries Bella Rosenfeld in Vitebsk.

1916 On 18 May, Chagall's daughter Ida is born.

1918 Chagall is appointed Commissar for the Fine Arts in Vitebsk.

1920 Chagall goes to Moscow, where he designs large murals for the Jewish Theatre.

1921 Chagall begins his autobiography "My Life".

1922 Chagall leaves Russia for good and travels to Berlin.

1923 On 1 September, Chagall arrives back in Paris again.

1924 Chagall is invited by André Breton to join the Surrealists, but refuses.

1927 A contract with the Parisian gallery Bernheim-Jeune guarantees him a livelihood.

1929 The Wall Street crash forces Bernheim-Jeune to terminate its contract with Chagall.

1931 Spends some months in Palestine.

1933 At the Mannheim Kunsthalle, a number of Chagall's works are publicly burned by the Nazis.

Biographie

Biographie

1887	Marc Chagall wird am 7. Juli als Moische Segal in Liosno bei Witebsk geboren.
1906	Chagall tritt in die Kunstschule des Malers Jehuda (Juri) Pen ein.
1907	Umzug nach St. Petersburg. Aufnahme in die Malerschule der Kaiserlichen Gesellschaft zur Förderung der Künste.
1908	Chagall studiert einige Monate an der Privatschule des Malers Sawel M. Saidenberg.
1909	Chagall wechselt zur liberalen Swansewa-Schule. Er lernt Bella Rosenfeld kennen, die sechs Jahre später seine Ehefrau wird.
1910	Besuch der Akademien La Palette und La Grande Chaumière in Paris.
1911	Chagall siedelt in das Atelierhaus La Ruche (Bienenkorb) in Paris über.
1912	Mit drei Gemälden beteiligt sich Chagall am Salon des Indépendants.
1914	Erste Einzelausstellung in der Berliner Galerie »Der Sturm«. Mit einem für drei Monate gültigen Reisepaß reist er von Berlin aus nach Rußland. Der Ausbruch des Ersten Weltkriegs verhindert die geplante Rückkehr nach Paris.
1915	In Witebsk heiratet Chagall Bella Rosenfeld.
1916	Am 18. Mai wird Chagalls Tochter Ida geboren.
1918	Ernennung zum Kommissar für die schönen Künste in Witebsk.
1920	Übersiedlung nach Moskau. Große Wandgemälde für das dortige Jüdische Theater.
1921	Beginn seiner Autobiographie »Mein Leben«.
1922	Chagall verläßt Rußland endgültig und reist nach Berlin.
1923	Am 1. September kehrt Chagall nach Paris zurück.
1924	Die Einladung André Bretons, sich den Surrealisten anzuschließen, lehnt Chagall ab.
1927	Ein Vertrag mit der Galerie Bernheim-Jeune sichert ihm seinen Lebensunterhalt.
1929	Der Börsenkrach an der Wall Street zwingt Bernheim-Jeune, den Vertrag mit Chagall aufzulösen.
1931	Mehrmonatige Palästinareise.

1887	Marc Chagall (Moyshe Segal) naît le 7 juillet à Liosno près de Vitebsk.
1906	Chagall commence des études à l'école d'art du peintre Jehouda (Juri) Pen.
1907	Déménagement à Saint-Pétersbourg. Intègre l'école de peinture de la Société impériale pour la protection des beaux-arts.
1908	Suit des cours privés à l'école du peintre Savel M. Saidenberg pendant quelques mois.
1909	Chagall entre à l'école libérale Zvanseva. Il fait la connaissance de Bella Rosenfeld qu'il épousera six ans plus tard.
1910	Chagall poursuit ses études dans les académies La Palette et La Grande Chaumière à Paris.
1911	Chagall s'installe à l'atelier de La Ruche, à Paris.
1912	Participe avec trois peintures au Salon des Indépendants
1914	Première exposition individuelle à la galerie berlinoise « Der Sturm ». Avec un visa pour trois mois, il se rend en Russie à partir de Berlin ; la Première Guerre mondiale l'empêche de retourner à Paris.
1915	À Vitebsk, Chagall épouse Bella Rosenfeld.
1916	Le 18 mai, naissance de sa fille Ida.
1918	Chagall est nommé commissaire pour les beaux-arts à Vitebsk.
1920	Chagall s'installe à Moscou où il réalise des grandes peintures murales pour le Théâtre Juif.
1921	Il commence son autobiographie « Ma Vie ».
1922	Chagall quitte définitivement la Russie et se rend à Berlin.
1923	Le 1er septembre, il retourne à Paris.
1924	André Breton invite Chagall à rejoindre le cercle des surréalistes, mais il refuse.
1927	Un contrat avec la galerie Bernheim-Jeune lui assure des revenus réguliers.
1929	Le krach boursier de Wall Street contraint Bernheim-Jeune à résilier le contrat avec Chagall.
1931	Voyage en Palestine pour quelques mois.

Marc Chagall painting *Solitude*, 1933–1934
Marc Chagall malt *Die Einsamkeit*
Marc Chagall peignant *Solitude*

Marc Chagall in front of the tapestry *The Entry into Jerusalem*
made for the Knesset in Jerusalem (ill. p. 24–25), c. 1969
Marc Chagall vor der tapisserie *Der Einzug in Jerusalem* für die
Knesset in Jerusalem (Abbildung S. 24–25), um 1969
Marc Chagall devant la tapisserie *L'Entrée à Jérusalem* (illustra-
tion p. 24–25), réalisée pour la Knesset à Jérusalem, vers 1969

1935	Trips to Vilna and Warsaw.
1936	Chagall moves into a new studio in Paris. Frequent encounters with Picasso.
1937	On the orders of the Nazi regime, all Chagall's works are removed from German museums. Chagall becomes a French citizen.
1939	Just before the outbreak of war, Chagall moves with his family to the relative safety of Saint-Dyé-sur-Loire.
1940	The Chagalls move to the South of France. Invitation to the United States.
1941	On 23 June, the Chagalls reach New York.
1942	Chagall spends the summer in Mexico.
1944	While staying at their summer house on Cranberry Lake, New York State, Bella catches a virus infection that kills her.
1945	Virginia Haggard becomes Chagall's housekeeper and later his lover and companion.
1946	On 22 June, Virginia Haggard gives birth to their son David.
1948	Chagall returns to France for good.
1950	In the spring, Chagall moves to Vence.
1951	Chagall travels to Israel for the opening of a retrospective in Jerusalem.
1952	Chagall meets Valentina (Vava) Brodsky, whom he marries on 12 July.
1960	Chagall starts work on stained-glass windows for the synagogue of the Hadassah Hebrew university clinic in Jerusalem.
1964	Chagall meets Yvette Cauquil-Prince, who completes her first Chagall tapestry one year later.
1966	Chagall and Vava move from Vence to neighbouring Saint-Paul-de-Vence.
1967	Retrospectives organised in Zurich and Cologne to mark Chagall's 80th birthday.
1968	Monumental wall mosaic for the University of Nice.
1971–1972	Designs for mosaics in Nice and Chicago.
1973	First trip to Russia after 50 years.
1977	Chagall is awarded the Grand Cross of the Legion of Honour by the French president.
1978–1979	Unveiling of stained-glass windows in Mainz, Chichester and Chicago.
1985	On the 28 March, Chagall dies at his home in Saint-Paul-de-Vence, aged 97.

1933	In der Mannheimer Kunsthalle werden mehrere Werke Chagalls von den Nazis öffentlich verbrannt.	1933	Plusieurs œuvres de Chagall sont publiquement brûlées par les nazis à la Kunsthalle de Mannheim.
1935	Reise nach Wilna und Warschau.	1935	Voyage à Vilnius et à Varsovie.
1937	Auf Anweisung des Naziregimes werden alle Arbeiten Chagalls aus deutschen Museen entfernt. Chagall wird französischer Staatsbürger.	1937	Sur ordre du régime nazi, toutes les œuvres de Chagall sont retirées des musées allemands. Chagall devient citoyen français.
1939	Kurz vor Kriegsausbruch zieht Chagall mit seiner Familie nach Saint-Dyé-sur-Loire.	1939	Peu avant que la guerre n'éclate, Chagall et sa famille s'établissent à Saint-Dyé-sur-Loire.
1940	Die Chagalls ziehen nach Südfrankreich in den Ort Gordes. Einladung in die USA.	1940	Les Chagall s'installent à Gordes, dans le Sud de la France. Invitation à se rendre aux États-Unis.
1941	Am 23. Juni erreichen die Chagalls New York.	1941	Ils arrivent à New York le 23 juin.
1942	Chagall verbringt den Sommer in Mexiko.	1942	Chagall passe l'été au Mexique.
1944	Bei einem Sommeraufenthalt in Cranberry Lake im Staat New York stirbt Bella überraschend an einer Virusinfektion.	1944	Lors d'un séjour estival à Cranberry Lake, dans l'État de New York, Bella meurt subitement d'une infection virale.
1945	Virginia Haggard wird seine Haushälterin und später seine Lebensgefährtin.	1945	Virginia Haggard devient la gouvernante de Chagall et sera plus tard sa compagne.
1946	Am 22. Juni bringt Virginia Haggard den gemeinsamen Sohn David zur Welt.	1946	Le 22 juin, Virginia Haggard met au monde leur fils David.
1948	Chagall kehrt endgültig nach Frankreich zurück.	1948	Chagall rentre définitivement en France.
1950	Im Frühjahr zieht Chagall nach Vence.	1950	Au printemps, Chagall s'installe à Vence.
1952	Chagall lernt Valentina (Vava) Brodsky kennen, die er am 12. Juli heiratet.	1952	Chagall fait la connaissance de Valentina (Vava) Brodsky, qu'il épouse le 12 juillet.
1960	Beginn der Arbeit an den Glasfenstern für die Synagoge des Klinikums der Hebräischen Universität Hadassah in Jerusalem.	1960	Commence les vitraux de la synagogue du « Medical Center » de l'université hébraïque Hadassah à Jérusalem.
1964	Chagall begegnet Yvette Cauquil-Prince, die ein Jahr später ihre erste Chagall-Tapisserie vollendet.	1964	Chagall fait la connaissance d'Yvette Cauquil-Prince qui achèvera un au plus tard sa première tapisserie d'après une œuvre du maître.
1966	Chagall und Vava ziehen von Vence in das benachbarte Saint-Paul-de-Vence.	1966	Chagall et Vava quittent de Vence pour Saint-Paul-de-Vence.
1967	Retrospektiven in Zürich und Köln anläßlich Chagalls 80. Geburtstag.	1967	Rétrospectives à Zurich et Cologne à l'occasion des 80 ans de Chagall.
1968	Monumentales Wandmosaik für die Universität Nizza.	1968	Monumentale mosaïque murale pour l'université de Nice.
1971–1972	Entwürfe für Mosaiken in Nizza und Chicago.	1971–1972	Réalise des mosaïques à Nice et Chicago.
1973	Erste Reise nach Rußland nach 50 Jahren.	1973	Premier voyage en Russie après 50 ans.
1977	Vom französischen Staatspräsidenten wird Chagall das Große Kreuz der Ehrenlegion verliehen.	1977	Chagall est nommé grand-croix de la Légion d'honneur par le président de la République française.
1978–1979	Einweihung verschiedener Glasfenster in Mainz, Chichester und Chicago.	1978–1979	Inauguration de différents vitraux à Mayence, Chichester et Chicago.
1985	Im Alter von 97 Jahren stirbt Marc Chagall am 28. März in seinem Haus in Saint-Paul-de-Vence.	1985	Le 28 mars, à l'âge de 97 ans, Marc Chagall s'éteint dans sa maison de Saint-Paul-de-Vence.

COVER/UMSCHLAG/COUVERTURE:
The Dance, 1997
Der Tanz
La Danse
Tapestry, 261 x 200 cm
Private collection

BACK COVER/UMSCHLAGRÜCKSEITE/DOS DE COUVERTURE:
The Creation, 1971
Die Schöpfung
La Création
Tapestry, 256 x 186 cm
Private collection

FRONT FLAP/KLAPPE VORN/JAQUETTE DE DEVANT:
The Entry into Jerusalem, (detail) 1963–1964
Der Einzug in Jerusalem (Detail)
L'Entrée à Jérusalem (détail)
Tapestry, 475 x 528 cm
Jerusalem, The Knesset

BACK FLAP/KLAPPE HINTEN/JAQUETTE DE DOS:
The Harlequin Family (detail), 1993
Die Harlekinfamilie (Detail)
La Famille d'Arlequins (détail)
Tapestry, 317 x 527 cm
Private collection

ILLUSTRATION P. 1/ABBILDUNG S. 1/ILLUSTRATION P. 1:
Animal Tales (detail), 1991
Tiererzählungen (Detail)
Le Bestiaire (détail)
Tapestry, 420 x 435 cm
Private collection

ILLUSTRATION p. 2/ABBILDUNG S. 2/ILLUSTRATION P. 2:
Marc Chagall, 1966
Photo: Darius Cauquil

© 1999 Benedikt Taschen Verlag GmbH
Hohenzollernring 53, D–50672 Köln
© 1999 VG Bild-Kunst, Bonn
Layout and editing: Bettina Ruhrberg, Cologne
Cover design: Angelika Taschen, Cologne
German translation: Wolfgang Himmelberg, Düsseldorf
French translation: Martine Passelaigue, Munich

Printed in Spain
ISBN 3–8228–6609–1